GURUS and **PSYCHICS** and **SHRINKS, OH MY!**

California Dreaming and Primal Screaming

JIMMY RYAN

NEW HAVEN PUBLISHING LTD

Published 2025

First Edition
NEW HAVEN PUBLISHING LTD
www.newhavenpublishingltd.com
newhavenpublishing@gmail.com

Cover design © George Foster

newhaven
publishing

Acknowledgments

To Maharishi Mahesh Yogi for introducing Transcendental Meditation to me and to the world.

To Neelam for her wisdom and love at a time when I needed it most.

To Adyashanti for his incredible intellect, insight and sense of humor, when teaching about spirituality.

To my wife, Gitam, for her patience, proofreading, and wise suggestions for the final version of this book.

To George Foster for his friendship, great bass playing and a killer cover design

To Werner Erhard (EST) for his breakthrough teachings about responsibility.

To John Hanley (Lifespring) for softening the blow I received from Werner Erhard's breakthrough teachings.

To Dr. Yvette Obadia for her tough love and showing me it's not always my fault.

To Dr. Barbara Larkin for volunteering her exceptional editing ability to see the bigger picture and apply it to telling me to get rid of a few passages that might get me in trouble.

To Teddie Dahlin for giving me the opportunity to share the second half of my story with the world.

Table of Contents

Introduction

In my first book, The Superstar Chronicles, I gave a ringside view of what it was like to work with some of the biggest recording stars of the sixties, seventies, and eighties. I provided an opportunity to ride with me on the tour bus, chill in the green rooms, stand on the stage in front of thousands of screaming fans and sit in the soundproof booth with me while I recorded guitar parts on songs like "You're So Vain," with Carly Simon and Jim Croce's, "You Don't Mess Around With Jim," as well as sessions with Paul McCartney, Rod Stewart, Cat Stevens, John Entwistle of the Who, Elton John & Kiki Dee, Tommy James, Jimmy Webb, The Doors, and many others. I gave you a blow-by-blow view of what it's like to perform with and induct someone into the Rock 'n Roll Hall of Fame, walk the red carpet, and mingle with legendary stars like Dolly Parton, Duran Duran, and Bruce Springsteen.

What I didn't discuss in Superstar were the quiet moments — what it felt like when that fun and excitement ebbed, and there were no peak experiences pounding through my psyche to keep the bliss flowing. As we all know, so many in the entertainment industry turn to drugs and drink in those moments when the spotlights go out and the darkness rises.

Many like myself, despite having achieved much of what we set out to accomplish, still experienced long-term depression. For me, it started in the crib and continued through my sixties. As a result, I spent almost as much time trying to heal my inner disquiet as I did playing guitar.

What you're about to read is an often entertaining and sometimes mind-blowing adventure into my experiences with self-repair. It will not be a typical how-to manual with a long list of things you can do if you're dealing with anything like what I went through. Also, I have no intention of taking you on a gloom & doom confessional of misery, regret, crash, and redemption, like the VH1 series, *Behind the Music*.

Instead, I present a series of short stories that illustrate my experiences with a number of legitimate and some questionable self-help remedies. Some of these therapies are still universally available and quite effective. Others are part of history — systems that did not stand the test of time or the patience of their practitioners. I include the discontinued ones, because they were so popular and hooked so many people like myself into believing they were worthwhile. Then there are the ones that made the cut under the category of "WTF — Are you kidding me?" i.e., "Why would anyone want to do that?"

My trauma cure tour began in my late teens. I would have started earlier, but the often-hostile environment surrounding my youth necessitated staging a coverup. In the Chicago and Detroit suburbs where I lived until age thirteen, you'd want to keep emotional issues on the down low. Same in my family. Put a lid on it. Be tough. Be a man. I exemplified the zipped-up kid, skilled in the art of emotional avoidance. In those days, not ok was not ok. That's how we rolled.

Beyond my growing up in stoic surroundings, the forties and fifties in general were not so favorable for examining depression and neurosis. Before the sixties, psychiatric analysis carried an unfortunate stigma. Many believed psychiatrists only treated crazy people. The thought that I might be considered mentally ill terrified me, so hard pass on that solution, at least for the moment.

In the mid to late sixties, though, attitudes around mental health changed. The stigma of seeking help began to fade. People no longer shied away from seeing psychologists, astrologers, psychics, and spiritual teachers. Among rock 'n roll musicians, remedies like smoking pot and dropping acid became commonplace. I *mostly* stuck to the legal ones, and I'm happy to report that even the weird ones added their own unique contribution to solving the mystery of misery for me.

Though I delved deep into psychology and spirituality, I became neither a psychologist, a life coach, nor a spiritual teacher, save a short period when I taught Transcendental Meditation. I remain a musician, but I'm also a repair junky with a lifelong interest in how things work. After enduring my troubled childhood for as long as I could, I focused my fix-it passion on repairing my heart and soul. Upon awakening to the downside of not dealing with my internal dilemma, I set out on my self-help journey.

So, before the stories begin, I encourage you to hold this odd and sometimes unlikely collection, not as a manual for recovery, but rather as a menu for a variety of self-help treatments. Enjoy the tales as entertaining sources of ideas for reflection, rather than specific courses of action to solve your problems. In *The Superstar Chronicles* I gave you a tour of what it's like to be an accompanist to the stars. In this book, I'll take you on a mental repair tour through some popular psychological healing techniques, some obscure ones and some flat-out, batshit crazy ones. Regarding the more bizarre encounters, I give you my word, I neither exaggerate nor fabricate.

As an introduction to why I set out on this journey, I'll begin with religion. Because I spent my formative years as a captive catholic, I not only suffered from life's normal circumstances; I suffered from a family-required faith that embraced several horror movie scare tactics. As a result, even following the rules, I spent my days and nights cycling between high and low-grade fear and anxiety.

The following chapter tells the story of my resignation from organized religion and my subsequent journey back to clarity. For my religious readers, please don't be put off by the idea of leaving one's faith. I'm not suggesting you do so. I simply distinguish between breaking from an organized religion and breaking from God. In my experience, one can ease up on religious dogma and still maintain a healthy, even improved relationship with the Almighty. Agnostics and atheists might take the extra step of throwing out the baby with the bath water. So far, I have not taken that step.

Message from the East
The Little Book That Changed Everything

A few hours of kicking back on this autumn Sunday afternoon gawking at the boob tube left me stiff, bored, and ready to roll off the couch. Time to move my lazy bones. A visit to my local bookstore seemed a good way to nudge my heart rate above fifty-five, so I switched off the TV, stretched, and grabbed the car keys. In those days I still lived with my parents, so to avoid my helicopter mom worrying about my whereabouts, I announced I was heading to Barnes & Noble, hopped in the car, and drove the half mile to the Americana Mall.

Few people shopped on Sunday in our little town, so I scored a parking place right in front of the store. I wandered in with no preference in mind, browsing and killing time, and soon found myself in the comparative religion section. Christian and Jewish books lined most of the shelves, but then an odd title caught my eye — a book called Hinduism. I said to myself, with a mischievous grin, "Now that's a word we don't toss around much at the dinner table." So, of course, I pulled this little paperback off the shelf and flipped through it. Gods and goddesses, like Lakshmi, Saraswathi, Indra, Brahma, Vishnu, Radha, and Krishna, filled the pages and sparked my curiosity. Did I stumble upon a heathen book of the false and forbidden? I could sense my Catholic guilt rising with every viewed page. The nuns of my youth used to warn us only one God ruled heaven and earth, but this book seemed to suggest there were many. To add to the confusion, the good sisters insisted we also embrace the three-in-one conundrum — God the Father, God the Son, and God the Holy Ghost, all the same God. Hinduism sold no such myth. They espoused an impressive family of heavenly rulers, each with their own specialty.

Of course, I bought the book, eager to learn about this intriguing and forbidden view of the unseen universe. And like an idiot, I took it home and showed it to my mom. With a furrowed brow reminiscent of the Spanish Inquisition, she sat me down, demanding I answer why I would waste my money and risk damning my soul on non-Catholic religious books. (Note: In my day, the Church forbade Catholics from attending non-Catholic congregations or reading non-Catholic religious texts under pain of mortal sin). Then, she reminded me of my altar boy days and how, for a while, I wanted to be a priest. Mom carefully left out the celibacy bit and its influence on my decision to do nothing of the kind. With a mocking, almost threatening tone, she suggested Hindu books make excellent fuel for bonfires. How do you make a book irresistible? Threaten to burn or ban it. She hoped that would be the end of it, but her myopic taunt backfired. My curiosity exploded into obsession.

The discovery of this unusual little paperback buried in the remote shelves of my local bookstore started me questioning everything my birth religion taught me about life and death — such a minor event, but so powerful. A mysterious and unforgettable treasury of gods, goddesses and living saints revealed itself within those pages — a new world outside the walled garden of Catholicism. I found myself fascinated, not so much by the folklore and myths, but because the book presented the possibility that millions, maybe billions of people held beliefs that differed substantially from mine.

After spending some time with the book, I realized embracing Hinduism, or any other "ism" would only replace one trove of magical thinking with another. I needed to bust out of my religious straight jacket altogether. So, I packed my mental bags, got into my mental car, floored my mental gas pedal, and crashed through the gates of my mental prison.

One afternoon, in my dorm at Villanova University (a Catholic institution), a friend asked me, "What are you doing? Why would you want to break away from our religion? Are you nuts? You could go to hell for this!"

I told him, "All my life, zealot priests and nuns had beaten the do-or-be-damned rules of behavior and beliefs into my naïve little brain until I wanted to scream. I'm drowning in dogma and need to dry out for a while."

With this reconning, Catholicism slipped from being the only way, to one of many ways. I will add, it now moved to the top of my list of no longer my ways. For me, religion caused more problems than it solved. You disagree? Ok, open up a religious discussion among friends of different faiths, and time how long it takes for the conversation to devolve from polite disagreement to bedlam.

Our beliefs divide us — we Catholics (or Jews, Muslims, etc.) stand righteous, the fervent purveyors of "truth" on God's side, and everybody else on the other side, the ignorant slugs. Why would anyone in their right mind call these isolationist, self-righteous points of view solutions to anything? Consider their results — the Crusades, the Spanish Inquisition, predator priests on the prowl, the ongoing conflicts between the Jews and the Muslims, terrorism, 911, etc., all in the name of a loving God.

Religion-based confusion presented just one of the many ongoing crises for me in my youth. I grew up in a "normal" family, and everything we espoused confirmed our status as mainstream American-OK. But I was not OK. I had been taught that powerful men don't display or talk about their insecurities or feelings, and because they pass that ignorance down through the generations, neither do their sons. With all of this patriarchal and religious craziness being fed into my little brain, supernatural and satanic fears began to haunt me. Nightmares about being pursued by monsters plagued me. Malevolent ghosts haunted my imagination. Vampires and the evil dead would rise from their graves at sundown and somehow make their way past our family dog and slip under my bed or into my closet.

My challenges didn't end there. Thick glasses and my skinny, non-athletic frame caused me no end of self-loathing. In my warped imagination, "unattractive" would be my yearbook description, not much else. And because we moved so many times with my dad's job, I found little opportunity to establish lasting friendships. (I apologize for all the gloom. I only mention the challenges to emphasize why I was so profoundly motivated to improve these unacceptable conditions.)

My life didn't stay horrible forever, though. Events took a turn in my late teens, and things started looking up. While struggling with all the above, my ill-begotten beliefs began to crumble. My suffering in silence, sharing my plight only in prayer with an ever-non-responsive Almighty, lost its appeal. Frightened and lonely, yes. Loser and a quitter, no. I didn't fade away into the shadows. With the help of that little Hindu book, I became a seeker, less focused on religion, and more focused on my dysfunctional family and my fears. My rebellious feelings ran deep. A new mindset/life direction now presented itself, and I embraced it with wild enthusiasm and determination.

Mental misery is like a multi-headed dragon, sometimes visible, most often hidden and almost always difficult to defeat, kind of like a real-world Game of Thrones with all the traps and monsters. Dear reader, don't let yourself be discouraged if you're going through any of what I've described above. I'll be giving you lots of ideas about how you might brighten up the dark spaces in your own life.

Two last incidents of note about religion and we'll move on. During my high school and college years, I would go to confession almost every Saturday evening. I was pretty sure I needed to. My girlfriend and I had become intimate, and *that*, the Church forbids! In fact, it is a mortal sin, punishable by endless torture, burning in hell. Out of white-knuckled fear, I confessed regularly. Interesting that simply telling a local priest what you did commutes the eternal damnation sentence to a few prayers. Then, off you go, free and clear.

It's Saturday night, confession night, and damnit, I'm next in line and the only confessional available is the one with the wrong priest. There's a line behind me and the other priest is occupied. My fate is sealed. I step up, open the door, enter, kneel, the door on the little window between the priest and the confessor (me), slides open and I take a deep breath. He can't see me because it's dark, he's looking the other way, and there's a semi-transparent veil between us. And so I begin:

"Bless me father for I have sinned. I French kissed my girlfriend. Umm... we're not married."

"What do you mean?

I give him a vague description that begins with, "You know..."

But he isn't letting me off the hook. He keeps asking me for more and more details.

"How far did your tongue go in? What did you feel when she responded? Did you touch her breasts or any other forbidden part of her body?"

"Noooo, nothing like that!" By this point, I'm not being entirely honest!

In his X-rated confessional, I feel like I'm dictating an article for Penthouse Magazine, and by the time we finish, I want to go home and take a shower. He is a creep, couldn't care less about my "sin," guilt or fear, but couldn't care more about hearing every intimate detail. Can you imagine being his altar boy? Needless to say, on future visits, I was more careful about calculating which confessional housed which priest. Eventually, I bagged the whole process. It no longer made sense, and was a golden opportunity for abuse.

The second incident was my last goodbye to The Church. Living on my own in NYC, my doubts continued to intensify. I decided to take a couple of questions to a priest and settle my issues once and for all.

I leave my 38th St. apartment, descend the six flights of stairs, step outside and take a walk to the RC Church a block away on the corner of Park and Madison. After a few knocks on the rectory door, a priest answers. I say,

"Father, I have a couple of pressing questions. Do you have a minute?"

"Of course, my son. How may I help?"

"Do you believe that God, in his infinite mercy and love, would send people to burn for all eternity if they simply slept in on a Sunday morning and missed mass?"

He sputtered, dodged, hedged, and finally said, "That is the teaching of Holy Mother Church, and yes, I believe that."

"Ok, with that answer, I only have one more question. We are no longer forbidden to eat meat on Fridays, correct?"

"Yes, correct. The Second Vatican Council relaxed that rule in 1966."

"So... do all those poor souls who downed a pig-in-a-blanket at the Friday afternoon office party get a reprieve from the burning flames and eternal torture of hell? Do they automatically get the equivalent of a presidential pardon? Do they rise out of hell in cinders and third-degree burns, to be immediately and miraculously healed, blissfully floating by Saint Peter through the pearly gates? (No, I didn't say all that, but you get the idea)

After a brief huffing and fumbling of words, he came up with, "These are decisions we leave up to God, so that is a question I cannot answer."

"But the Pope created this edict. It was a man-made rule in the first place. Now the rule has been rescinded. Are you telling me the Creator of the Universe takes orders from the Pope?"

This question annoys him. He realizes his position and the position of the "Holy See" are untenable. Without an answer, he says

"I am very busy, and it is time to end our little conversation."

And with that, I bid farewell to the Catholic religion; I did not dump God; just the organization that purports to represent Him.

The Relentless Mind

As a teaser, before we jump into my adventures in Dizzyland, I'd like to introduce an obvious, yet not-so obvious pest that will be a paramount player in all the following chapters — *the mind!* I've become fond of the phrase, "A mind is a terrible thing." I'm talking about the source of the cerebral machinations that tortured me daily. The mind can be a wonderful problem solver, an always-on app churning away on our brain-computers. Wouldn't it be nice if this often-annoying little chatterbox restricted its activity to things like solving math and remembering where we put the remote, instead of being an often miserable, whiny, gossiping, critical, judgmental, invisible hooligan? For me, no such filter existed in my busy little thinker. Instead, my mind was too often a persistent, annoying presence, rarely silent and always opinionated. I'd call this app running on a bundle of neurons, an uninvited narrator, commenting and questioning everything I did. I could distract myself, temporarily silencing its endless drivel, but soon I found it crouching in the shadows, ready to spring into a flurry of opinions as soon as the distraction faded. And I assumed this mind was *me*. After spending many years practicing meditation and yoga, I had to consider the possibility that not only is the mind not *me*, but its endless monolog might just be noise. Sometimes joyous noise, sometimes useful noise, sometimes terrible noise, but maybe even self-impersonating noise.

Most people use outward focused distraction to drown out their mental radio station, i.e. Facebook, TV, YouTube, news, politics, etc. My first successful band, The Critters, provided quite a substantial amount of that distraction in its active years, a welcome respite from this noise spewing dragon. But distraction is not always available. For instance, there were no fans, no spotlights, no cheering crowds when I would be lying in bed at night… just me and my demons singing me to sleep with self-deprecating lyrics. In those Catholic years, I sprinkled in prayers with the thoughts of failure, but they remained unanswered. Prayers would silence the critic, but only during the praying.

When I ran out of escapist strategies, or ran the clock out on a particular distraction, mental noise returned. As an EST trainer once said, "When we go on vacation, we don't leave our problems behind. We take a suitcase full of them with us, and they're more than happy to share our blankets at the beach." For me, distractions did not defeat demons. I could not dispatch them without intent, hard work, and self-reflection. They would lie waiting, ready to pounce the minute my attention drifted. And what about sex? Most of us have learned that our demons don't wait for the happy ending before expressing their opinions. Talk about a buzzkill. Anyone ever had a self-defeating thought during sex? I see a lot of hands up!

Ok, enough background. Let's get on with the stories! My first attempt at smacking down the multi-headed beast happened in the early seventies in NY City. I spent two years screaming my way back to sanity.

The Primal Scream

This story begins in Spring 1968. I'm twenty-one years old. Managing my unrelenting anxiety feels like trying to walk through three feet of snow with a fifty-mph headwind. But I'm determined to find a cure and release myself from this emotional numbness. A book called *The Fear of Freedom* by Erich Fromm catches my attention. Dr. Fromm explains that most people stay stuck in their self-destructive ways because they're afraid to abandon the familiar and embrace the unknown. No argument from me. I spent most of my youth as the poster boy for this theory, a functional stuckaholic. Getting unstuck seemed like a good place to start. But as I mentioned in the chapter on religion, examining beliefs was not an option in my family. Quite the opposite. Either a) one accepted the teachings of the Church, or b) face the fires of hell. I chose b), accepting the imaginary consequences. As that choice is working out well, it's unlikely I'll ask to be buried with a fire extinguisher.

So, about that ecclesiastical brainwashing making me want to scream... I didn't mean it literally, but then things changed.

It's Autumn 1968. I've left the safety of my parents' home in Westfield, NJ and moved to a beautiful apartment in the Murray Hill section of Manhattan on 38th St. I'm finally on my own, making my own decisions, and I couldn't be happier with my newfound freedom. Then the excitement starts. In the course of an average morning, I make a discovery that changes my life, even more than that little Hindu book. From my journal:

It's a beautiful Sunday morning. I get up, throw on some clothes, go downstairs, stroll across 38th and down Madison Ave. to the local deli for coffee and a bagel... and without thinking, I purchase a copy of the Sunday Times. I rarely bother with this almost comically oversized pile of verbal mulch, but something tells me today is a good day to do so. Hauling this mountain of paper up the six flights of stairs to my apartment, I remove some of the less interesting sections. Section 4, Politics is the first to go straight into the cat box. I'm out of kitty litter, so my cat, Pyewacket, will have to deal.

The front page has a large picture of Richard Nixon and nothing else eye-catching, so I leaf through the other sections looking for The Times Book Review. Despite my mediocre high school English grades, I'm an avid reader, excited to see what books might be catching those esteemed NYT editors' attention. As I scan the page, I spot an unusual title. A Dr. Arthur Janov has written a book called The Primal Scream — Primal Therapy, The Cure for Neurosis. I'm riveted. Without a shred of evidence other than a Times review, I decide this, not Catholicism, or Hinduism, or any other "ism" is what I've been searching for. Just the suggestion that screaming could be therapeutic triggered a welling up from the core of my being — anger, rage, anxiety, fear, and elation. But I'm in an apartment with neighbors, so I had to zip it... for now.

My reaction to this book review seems strange and unexpected, maybe a little frightening, and I find myself staring out the window for several minutes. Never have I experienced such a powerful reaction to a book review. I want this, and I want it now... but then practicality rears its ugly head. Dr. Janov practices in Beverly Hills, and I'm a mere up-and-coming musician with a yearly income of not Beverly Hills. Sad and disappointed, I table this fantasy and set to work to find an affordable alternative.

Fate intervened. During this time, I managed a store called Dan Armstrong Guitars, where I met a fellow guitarist named Charlie Brown (real name). He would often come around the store, hang out, and jam with us. One day, during a pause in our playing, I brought up the subject of primal screaming. Charlie jumped right into the conversation, as he read the Janov book too, and took the information one step further. A program on the Upper West Side called *Groups*, incorporated many of Janov's techniques. Charlie attended these sessions every week and suggested I check them out. I took down the address and phone number and before I left work, called to book an interview.

Dr. Stevens (made-up name, as I forgot his real name. Only met him once, fifty years ago), the psychologist in charge of screening applicants asked me several personal questions which I answered with, in his opinion, unusual sincerity. With nothing to hide and my limited experience in the realm of psychology, there seemed no reason to mistrust him. But his evaluation was so far off, it took me a minute to comprehend. In his opinion, I didn't need therapy.

He mistook my "I'm ok" act and enthusiastically hopeful responses for sanity. I assured him that under the hood, out of his sight, lived hideous monsters, evil and contriving, jealous and conniving, and my need for this therapy was at DEFCON 2!! With a peculiar half-smile and one raised eyebrow, he said, "Ok then," and signed off on my application. I was now an official client, as psychologists like to call us, and ready to brave whatever my subconscious might regurgitate, damn the consequences.

The following is a description of my first session. I expected to see and hear people spewing all kinds of crazy, but I was not prepared for this. Again, from my journal:

There are ten of us in this session, equally distributed between men and women. After brief introductions, our facilitator, Barbara Sher, lays out some general ground rules, and invites us to turn inward and get in touch with what's going on inside.

A middle-aged woman named Judy raises her hand and says, "I'd like to work." She tells us she recently lost her husband to cancer and pauses. With Barbara's coaching, Judy begins with eyes closed, slowly repeating the words, "I miss you, Tom," over and over. Tears stream down her cheeks and several of ours as she continues, "I miss you, baby, I miss you so much." Barbara encourages her to keep going, deeper and deeper. Now she's wailing. Three women members of the group chime in with support. Another woman is holding her hand. "I miss you, baby, I miss you so…" Then she suddenly stops and opens her eyes. Her face changes. A strange, severe presence has replaced the sad victim, and the tears are gone. To my shock, she says in a low, quiet, almost evil voice, "You fucking bastard. I fucking hate you." Louder — "I FUCKING HATE YOU! YOU LEFT ME TO MANAGE EVERYTHING, YOU FUCKING CREEP!" Barbara is on it, right there with her. For the rest of us, the room felt like it had morphed into a horror movie. Barbara yells, "Go with it, Judy! That's it! Right there! Scream it!!" Judy clenches her fists and slams her thighs as she screams. Barbara whisks a pillow onto her lap between blows, so she doesn't go home looking like she took second place in a gorilla fight. "FUCK YOU TOM!!! I HOPE YOU'RE IN FUCKING HELL!! HOW COULD YOU LEAVE ME LIKE THIS?? ASSHOLE!!"

Judy's screaming, fist pounding madness continued for who knows how long? Nobody was looking at their watches. I found myself churning through astonishment, wonder, and shock. The idea of contradictory layered feelings presented a whole new world to me. I must have read about it in *The Primal Scream,* but seeing it in action was a game changer. With Barbara's guidance and the group's encouragement, Judy transformed herself into a Marvel superhero, blasting through her trauma and opening to a deeper sense of kindness, understanding, and finally, peace.

This woman's bravery and willingness to expose her darkest emotions was an inspiration for the entire group. When the anger subsided, her face became clear and open. Some tears of sweetness were all that remained as she told her late husband she loved him, missed him, and wished him safe passage on his journey to the heavens. With this, the group crushed her with hugs and support. Barbara took the opportunity to give a brief talk about not holding back whatever comes up, no matter how odd or scary. She emphasized that there are no invalid feelings. Dismissing or editing emotions is counter-productive and self-sabotaging. Even if you're struggling to get out of a stuck moment, you keep going as long as your energy permits. Trigger phrases are key. The facilitator can be helpful, and sometimes the group members can make suggestions, but the individual has the ultimate responsibility to find words that dredge up those gut-wrenching feelings.

My group therapy friends always comforted me when my disturbing memories arose, never skimping on the love, hugs, and encouragement to go deeper. But from my side, there was a little problem. I enrolled in these sessions for my own evolution, not others. Most everyone begins in a self-oriented frame of mind, but in most cases, they evolve to be more compassionate to their group-mates. I remained stuck in "I'm here for me." Though I watched passively as everyone went through their dramas and traumas, I put little effort into comforting them. My participation began with my time on the mat. It wasn't malice; it was cluelessness.

Barbara, being an astute observer, lets me get away with my self-centered nonsense for a few sessions, but then one evening, she drops a bomb. After several tries getting to my feelings, I fail to come up with an activating trigger, so she stops me. "I believe it's time you joined this group, don't you?"

Her comment seems to come out of nowhere. Trying to decipher it while sweating and panting, I respond, "What are you talking about? I'm here! I'm participating!"

She continues, "The problem is you act like these sessions are only about you. You are wrong, and I have no interest in continuing with you until that changes. Look around. You need to acknowledge and be here for these amazing people, not just yourself."

After a half-hearted protest, I admitted she got me. True, I rarely hugged anyone, assisted no one and only commented when it was about me. But no problem shooting my hand up like an obnoxious little schoolboy at every opening in the proceedings. Compassion? What's that? Empathy? Not on my dime. With some embarrassment for acting like a jerk, I agreed to cut the selfish crap and show some compassion and respect.

Minutes after I made that commitment, I experienced a perspective shift. Concern about the people surrounding me started to creep in. Their pain became my pain. This simple change in attitude created an opening, and a part of me that felt dead got the paddles and came back to life. I had been navigating relationships without the aid of emotional radar, unable to sense the feelings and concerns of my friends and family until they boiled over. You might say I had a limited ability to read the room. This happened often enough that it became one of my primary reasons to seek help. Groups provided that help.

The encouragement of compassion and empathy was not part of my emotional education growing up. Groups provided a live, in-my-face demonstration of how powerful caring for others can be. With Barbara's tough love guidance, I learned that these two beautiful qualities unite us, that they are not weaknesses like I had been taught and had been demonstrated so often in my youth.

My primal period wasn't always histrionics and bedlam, though. Two amusing incidents occurred that are worth mentioning here.

We're now in Spring, 1972. It's Thursday evening, I arrive for our usual scheduled session, and a new member strolls in. This doesn't happen often, so when it does, we all perk up to see what's cooking.

The group then proceeds with the usual cacophony, and the new gentleman sits alert with arms folded, legs crossed, observing us screaming our guts out and acting like psychos. During a break in the action, to our surprise, this first-timer raises his hand. Newbies rarely do that, so he gets our undivided attention. This guy looks familiar... no way... I recognize him. As he mumbles his name, "Bob Klein." I think to myself, Klein! Holy crap, this is my 9th grade shop teacher. He gave me an "A" for a guitar amp I built that year!

I don't want to blow my cover. This process is hard enough without a former student in the room. I let him take his best shot at digging up some deep feelings without announcing my presence in the room. He doesn't do well — not surprising for a newbie. I remain incognito. We carry on with our caterwauling and pillow beating, and after an hour and a half of mayhem, the evening ends. Everyone gathers their belongings, we exchange hugs, and one by one, file out the door. I have Bob Klein in my sights and pounce,

"Hi there! You probably don't remember me, but I was your shop student in 1962. I loved you, man. You gave me an A for my yellow and brown guitar amp! You were my favorite teacher! So glad you're here!"

Talk about a deer in the headlights! Mr. Klein, as we were required to call him in class, nervously acknowledges that he at least remembers the amp. It's apparent that a hug is not on the table. He thrusts his manly hand in my direction, saying, "Nice to see you again, kid," and with a knuckle-crushing handshake, bolts out the door and vanishes into the night.

Not a touchy-feely guy, this Bob Klein. I'm guessing he'd be far more comfortable doing Jack Daniels therapy at his local bar than baring his soul to a room full of howling strangers. I'll never know if meeting him again was a portentous moment, or just one of those odd events that the universe concocts to mess with us. It was a cool guitar amp, though, and I deserved the A.

The next anomaly came a month later. Same scenario.

We all shuffle in, and at the end of the line is a stranger — a new person thinking they're ready for the wringer, but in fact, painfully unaware of what will ensue when they raise their hand. This time my recognition is instantaneous — that smug face, the swagger that says, "I'm a dick. Deal with it." I know this guy, and what I know is not good.

I wait like a Colorado mountain lion, laser-focused on my prey. The group does its usual rounds, as people share, one after another, and like Bob Klein, he surprises us by raising his hand.

"Hello. My name is Terry Slater."

He then delivers a litany of complaints about his wretched life, greedy wives, ungrateful kids, stressful job, blah, blah, blah. Like Bob, he can't get the emotional dredge going to any satisfying depth beyond annoyance, so after ten minutes, he gives up, and we move on.

The woman to my right finishes, and I'm up...

"Hi, Terry. My name is Jimmy, and this is not the first time we've met."

His eyes widen. Someone whispers, "Uh oh."

"A few years back, I belonged to a band called the Critters. We had a hit record called 'Don't Let the Rain Fall Down on Me.' You hired us to record a jingle using my song as the basis for a new one that you wrote for Fresca."

My tone is not friendly. I smile as he cringes.

"A musical phrase on your lead sheet contained some wrong notes in the opening. As the composer of the song and the expert in the room, I felt the need to correct it. You turned on me like a prison warden and said,

"This is my song, not yours, my session, not yours, my client, not yours, and if you know what's good for you, you'll keep your mouth shut and do as you're told."

"You insulted, humiliated, and embarrassed me in front of my band, the studio personnel, and the Fresca client."

Then I let it rip. "You fucking dick! Who the fuck do you think you are? You're not even a real musician. How dare you talk to me like that? I was the lead singer, guitarist, and composer of a hit record you appropriated for your stupid jingle, and you have the nerve to talk to me like a waiter who just spilled a bowl of soup in your lap? Go fuck yourself, asshole. I don't care about your miserable life. Shove it up your ass!!!"

I didn't need to repeat a single phrase. This one-stop trigger-fest opened the floodgates. When I concluded my rant, you could hear a pin drop in the room. My group-mates were afraid I was going to lunge and knock him over in his chair.

Terry buries his face in the palm of his hand and neither denies my accusations nor defends his actions. To everyone's astonishment, he apologizes:

"I know, I know, you're right. When things don't go my way, I lose my temper. Yes, I disrespected you and acted like an arrogant jerk. And for the record, you're not the first person to call me a dick. Get in line behind my family. I'm here to try and understand why I act that way. Please accept my sincere apology. You wrote a great song, the world loved it, and I had no right to talk to you that way."

Well, didn't that just drain the piss and vinegar out of my little tirade? It was an easy apology to accept. I said what I needed to say, and he humbly relented. Barbara and the group loved our interaction, and several people commented on the unexpected transformation that took place in both of us. If we were in a bar, our faces would have been transformed by broken beer bottles, but here, we both got to the depth of our feelings without violence. Unlike Bob Klein, Terry asked for a hug, and I was happy to stand and deliver.

Neither Terry Slater nor Bob Klein returned to Groups. We had seen the last of them, and this surprised no one. You need a lot of courage and commitment to take an extreme step like this and risk what you might discover about yourself. Some fear that what they uncover will drive them further into madness. In my two years at Groups, I never saw that happen. In fact, quite the opposite. I would say everyone made at least some progress, and for many, the change was remarkable.

My time with Groups ended shortly after these incidents. Just prior to my moving on, I made a rather extreme decision. My current life no longer interested me. I told Barbara I needed a significant change. London was calling. Having recently recorded there with Carly Simon, I fell in love with this amazing city. I wanted to move there… immediately. To my surprise, Barbara was all for it. She cheered me on and said it was a great life decision and was sure I would thrive there. I took it one step further. Before the session where I revealed my plan to her and the group, I called my parents and *resigned from my family*. In the next chapter, I'll describe the events that led up to this decision, but for now, it was done. Of course, my parents and the group were shocked, but my mom responded with a comment that assured me I made the right decision.

When I told her I was cutting the family loose and moving to London, her reaction was,

"Oh no, no... what will we tell our friends?"

Her concern was not losing her son. She was concerned that she would look like a failure to her friends. After that revelation, I ended the conversation with,

"I wish you well. Goodbye."

And that was it.

To conclude this chapter, I will say that Primal Therapy, or its offshoot, Groups, was one of the most enduring blessings along my road to sanity. With it, I uncovered a frozen mass of confusion and delusion in my being and blasted it to kingdom come. Would I recommend it to everyone? Only to those willing to face their fears with unshakable determination. It is not for the faint of heart, and some major changes in your attitude and life are almost guaranteed. Though it may not be for the masses, I can confidently say it changed my life. The memory of sharing that space on 94th St., and drubbing my demons with those wonderful, brave people, still shines like a bright light in my heart. To this day, I hold those two years to be among the most cherished and powerful phases of my self-development.

I would also like to express my heartfelt thanks to Barbara Sher. I was able to turn my life around with her guidance. Sadly, she left us on May 10, 2020 at 85, but not without making her mark on the world. From Wikipedia:

Barbara Sher was a speaker, career/lifestyle coach, and author. Her books have sold millions of copies

and were translated into many languages. She appeared on Oprah, The Today Show, 60 Minutes, CNN, and Good Morning America and her public television specials aired regularly in the United States. Sher lectured at universities, Fortune 100 companies and professional conferences all over the world.

Sarah's Foreshadowing

While living in New York City, working as a studio musician and Carly Simon's guitarist, I met a young woman named Sarah. She had previously dated James Taylor, Carly Simon's future (now ex) husband, so our paths conveniently crossed. Sarah had an interesting past. She was of Irish descent and had a very Gaelic sounding birth name. Not wishing to seem like a foreigner, she changed it to a very ordinary Anglicized one. I'm a proud Irishman, so I would often call her by her Gaelic name, which never failed to piss her off. She would retaliate by calling me by one of my male body parts.

We moved in together almost immediately. With Sarah being a hottie, I was willing to overlook the fact that the state of California designated her legally insane, or at least, that's what she claimed. She believed a psycho diagnosis gave her street cred and some tax advantages. I believed it gave me a solid reason to keep an eye on the kitchen cutlery. Sarah was also a strident singer-songwriter who accompanied herself with an autoharp. Listening to her shrill voice was about as pleasant as mike feedback, but again, she was a hottie, and I was a young, testosterone-laced musician, happy to ignore quite a lot for the exercise and satisfaction of my immature urges.

Sarah and I were a short-lived couple, none the least because her permanent residence and "old man" were somewhere in the Bay Area. She never told me exactly where, and I didn't press it. That plus one weekend she flew in, allegedly, to see *me*. It soon became clear I was not the person of interest this trip. Upon removing her coat, a pair of scissors revealed three bags of pure, uncut, pharmaceutical grade cocaine sewn into the lining. Over the weekend she dumped them into a big mixing bowl on my antique oak dining room table and cut (street slang for blended) the raw cocaine with lactose powder to stretch the quantity. Sarah, a rookie with no experience dealing or cutting, overdid the lactose, ruining the batch. She called a few people she thought might be interested in buying her powdered nonsense, but after their testing a line or two, the best they could offer was some belly laughs, followed by, "you must be kidding!" Not sure how she explained the spoiled lot to her supplier, but I can't imagine it went well.

Why am I bringing Sarah up and telling you all of this? Just an intro to how I discovered meditation, which I will detail shortly. I lived in a large studio apartment with a sleeping loft. From the bed, you could only see half the apartment, while the other half was under the loft. I woke up one morning and Sarah wasn't in bed. Had she left? I heard not a peep in the apartment, save the muffled sound of cars and trucks passing on 38th Street downstairs. I descended the loft stairs to see her sitting on the floor, cross-legged, eyes closed and utterly silent. Epileptic Seizure? Paralysis? I wasn't quite ready to call the paramedics, so I tiptoed into the kitchen and brewed a pot of coffee as quietly as I could. About five minutes later, she slipped silently into the kitchen, surprising me. She looked beautiful and quite peaceful as she leaned in to give me a kiss. Sarah's normally chaotic personality was nowhere to be found. I asked, "what were you doing in there? You look amazing."

"Transcendental Meditation."

"What's that?"

She described it as sitting in a comfortable position with eyes closed and silently repeating a mantra. It looked more like rigor mortis to me, but I remained curious.

"Why? What does that do?"

"It clears my head and calms me down. It's also supposed to raise your consciousness. I don't know about that, but it just makes me feel better."

"Interesting…where did you learn how to do it? Can you teach me?"

"No. I think you need a qualified instructor to give you your own personal mantra. Mine probably wouldn't work for you. They're kind of like needles — you don't exchange them, because you don't know what will happen. They teach it in San Francisco, though."

That was the end of my curiosity. If it wasn't available in New York, I had little interest. Apparently, there was a TM center in Greenwich Village (NYC), but discovering it would have required my picking up the Yellow Pages and looking it up. For a diehard sanity seeker, I credit myself with some shameful laziness on that one. I gave TM no further thought, at least not in that moment.

After about a month, I realized that Sarah and I were a bad match. Did I mention she believed in polyamory and hit on a couple of my friends while living with me? For her, this was completely acceptable. She called it free love. I called it free rent while cheating. Upon the dissolution of our shallow romance, she moved back to the Bay Area, and that was that.

Strain in the Studio

Crying in Cornwall

F ast forward to 1973. I spent two summers in London playing guitar, bass and backing vocals on Carly Simon's *Anticipation* album in 1971, then her *No Secrets* album ("You're So Vain") in 1972. As I mentioned in the Primal Chapter, in 1973 I had reached an untenable situation with my parents, and in a somewhat rash moment of anger and sadness, I resigned from my family. After that I needed a big change of environment, and it became my dream to move to London. The nightlife, the culture, the European vibe, the history — hooked and intoxicated, I had to go. I was also in my early twenties, a tad short on common sense, obsessed with British women and their sexy accents, and, as I may have mentioned, a tad long on testosterone. But I needed a solid reason above and beyond yearning, and a job to avoid becoming homeless once I got there.

The solution fell out of the sky. While working on *No Secrets* during that summer, I received a job offer from a very unlikely source. One of Carly's roadies, Richie Gerstein, was also visiting London, and he was a sleuth extraordinaire. He had no qualms about sticking his nose into places of opportunity, both invited and uninvited, and one of those places was WEA, Warner Bros./Elektra/Atlantic, the British division of Carly's record company. Richie got wind of a hot new band from New Zealand, currently being signed and looking for a producer.

He did not suggest I apply for the job; he applied for me without telling me, got the project head interested and handed me his phone contact at a party. I would have accepted a job producing a banjo mandolin band if it would get me a residency in London, so I made an appointment, went up and met with Jonathan Clyde (brother of Jeremy Clyde, of Chad & Jeremy) who was the project head, and by coincidence, the label rep for Carly. We chatted about my resume, our mutual friends, and with minimal negotiation, sealed the deal.

We had finished *No Secrets*, so I extended my stay in London for a month to get the ball rolling with this project, a kick-ass band known as Bitch. Now it was time to decide. Do I continue extending my visa to finish the project, or do I go home, gather my belongings and move to London? I chose B. Having resigned from my family, there was nothing holding me in the US. The UK beckoned to the free spirit I had become, and I answered the call.

Again, you would be well to ask what all of this has to do with self-development. We'll get there. I've learned over the years that damn near everything in our lives affects our self-development, none-the-least a move to a foreign country to take a job with a band from yet another foreign country, and produce their album, something I had never done before and had just bullshitted my way into doing! Fake it 'til you make it seemed to be the call of the moment.

So now I've moved not to London but Crowborough, Sussex, England, 2.5 hrs. South of London to live with my new band-wards, the Bitch. We occupy this delightful five-bedroom estate in a rural but fancy neighborhood, and we're getting on great. Every day we convene in the practice room, plug in and go through the songs, one by one, fine-tuning them, organizing the arrangements, rehearsing the vocals, eliminating the unnecessary or long solos and turning these songs into hits... we hope. The band dynamic is well-balanced — a brother and sister lead singer combo, Ron and Gaye Brown, a lyric writing bass player, Rob Aickin, and a quiet but rock-solid drummer, Ace Follington... and me... the Yank who showed up on their doorstep, like an Amazon package they didn't order, to move in and teach them how to make hit records.

Does it sound like a dream job in a dream setting? When we were working at home and in the studio, it was. But then there loomed the downtime, and plenty of it. Though we developed solid friendships that remain in place to this day, I spent a lot of time alone in that house. I don't do alone well — never did, probably never will. During that time, I damn near wore out my copy of the I Ching. For those unfamiliar, the I Ching is a compilation of ancient Chinese wisdom, an oracle of sorts, consulted using coins or yarrow stalks. From holisticshop.co.uk:

The I Ching is the world's oldest oracle; it's a book of Chinese wisdom and the accumulated experience of over 2,500 years of diviners and sages, and beyond that of unimaginably ancient oral traditions. The I Ching is the voice that has been offering people help and wise, genial guidance for generations.

Worry and confusion had me putting my conscious, doubt-filled, discriminating mind on pause, consulting this Chinese oracle daily, asking for advice, and trying to discern why I felt like absolute crap under such ideal circumstances. I received many answers to my endless queries, always in the form of cryptic aphorisms, but words are not solutions. Solutions require action, and despite my voracious reading and oracle consulting, I still had no solid, reliable compass to guide me to what I imagined to be the promised land, i.e. peace, contentment and happiness. So, the pursuit continued unabated.

I remember when we finished the Bitch album, the lads (and lady) had a friend from New Zealand coming to stay. In their words, "Sorry mate. You'll have to move out. The album's done, and we need the room." Of course, I didn't expect to live with them forever, but this news hit me hard. Where would I go? I'm alone, the proverbial stranger in a strange land. Well, first off, I had imported my car from the US, a nice 1966, 911 Porsche, so at least I was mobile. What do you do when you're an ex Primal Therapy client who just got evicted? Why, you get in your car, drive like the wind, and find a secluded place to scream until you hurl out the last drop of negative or painful emotion. My choice of destination was Cornwall in Southwest England. Here's how it went:

I've been driving for six hours, and I'm feeling hopeless and lost. I've got to dissipate this anguish, and this is the place for it. As I cruise along the Cornish coast, a sign appears ahead, "Penzance 10 Km," and beyond it I spot a deserted beach. This road has wide shoulders, so I pull over and shut off the engine. For a moment, I just sit staring at the ocean. There is a reason I came here, but I fear what will happen if I let go. Neither Barbara Sher nor my group is here to rescue me and hold my hand if I lose control, but no way am I going to back down. This is it. I'm going for it.

I open the car door and step out. The chill breeze blowing off the ocean hits my face, and I take a deep breath. There's an opening to the beach, across the road and about ten yards ahead, so I approach, slip sideways down the steep incline to the rocks and sand. A flat-topped boulder facing the water lies a few yards away, so I walk to it and sit down. My time has come. Primal rage and anguish well up inside me and I begin to cry my eyes out, shouting the words over and over, "Goodbye, mommy," "Goodbye daddy," "I will never see you again." My crying turns to howling, then screaming. I feel like I'm losing my mind, and in some ways, I am, but I don't care, and I don't stop.

I must have sat there for an hour or more, fading in and out of despair, peace, and occasionally touching on hope. It is well-documented that periods of complete solitude in the right environment can help to dredge up and resolve negative feelings and trauma that would be difficult to exhume any other way, and on this day, I was living proof. It was both cathartic and reassuring that I had done the right thing, both resigning from my family and coming here to resolve the feelings that led to that declaration of independence.

From here, feeling relief and a modicum of self-confidence, I headed straight to the nearest pub and raised a pint or two with some locals who seemed fascinated with this wild-haired, Porsche driving musician from across the pond, motor-mouthing absurd stories about resolving trauma and agony by screaming.

My (to them) phantasmal rants were met with,

"Ye did wha?" "No, mate, that's looney! Why would ye wanna do any of thet? And what did yer ma and pa have to say about yer wacky notions? You're a right nutter by my measure, but I like a good story as much as the next bloke! Oy, barman! Pull the Yank another pint. Looks like we're gonna be here a while!"

London Marriage

Before I left Crowborough, I made a call to my friend Dan Armstrong, the legendary guitar maker and my ex-boss, who now lived in London, to see if he knew of any available apartments. In England and Ireland, there is a lodging phenomenon called "bedsitter." It's usually one room in a house with a bed, a table, maybe a dresser and access to a bath, toilet and hopefully something resembling a kitchen. In most cases, the rent is reasonable, paid by the week, no lease, come and go as you please, and an opportunity for some companionship from the owner and other tenants. Dan said that by coincidence, his friend and business partner had a room that just opened up in his house in West Hampstead, London, and would be happy to rent it to me.

After completing my hard bawl and pub crawl in Cornwall, I started the six-hour trek up to London. Not much to tell about the journey other than it was as majestic and beautiful going as coming. When I arrived at 34 Hillfield Road, West Hampstead, I was met by Tucker and Maggie, the homeowners who led me to my room which sat adjacent to the front entrance. Tucker opened the room door, revealing a pine-paneled, high ceiling, fifteen by twenty room, with shelves and bookcases, a comfortable bed, a roomy closet, accessible to a full kitchen down a flight of stairs, and a full bath at the top of the other stairs. This would be my new London home, but only for a few short months. Why? Because Tucker and

Maggie were on the outs, and while he was on the road with his band, Maggie chose my shoulder to cry on. When he found out, he was neither amused nor sympathetic, so both Maggie and I left the house on Hillfield Road, me for an apartment on Hampstead Heath, her for a bedsitter about two blocks away. As you might be thinking, the shoulder crying evolved, and before long, Maggie abandoned her bedsitter and took up residence in my apartment. Our relationship took off, and a year later, we tied the knot.

While we're on the subject of weddings, it had been two years since I resigned from my family. After living in London for that time, most of my anger and resentment towards my parents had subsided. As a gesture of good faith, and knowing from my brother and sisters how hurt everyone was by my sudden and unexpected decision to leave the fold, I invited mom and dad to the wedding. To my surprise, they accepted, and flew to England for the happy occasion. They stayed for two weeks, which gave us lots of time to talk about what led up to my resignation, and they were unusually understanding. Once we all accepted our individual roles in the problem, we exchanged apologies and did our best to move on.

I was happy we reunited, and apologies go a long way towards healing old wounds, but there was no denying, our relationship had changed. We were cordial, like friends, but the closeness I had always hoped for was not to be. I respect that their life was not easy, also growing up in dysfunctional families, and I was satisfied that they were able to admit that our relationship was not as ideal as they had convinced themselves.

From then on, we returned to spending all the usual family holidays together, talked on the phone from time to time, and on the surface, it appeared that all was well. But for me, all was not yet well. Primal therapy went a long way towards improving my ability to function normally, but I still struggled with some remaining psychological issues. With steadfast determination to find peace, my journey continued.

Transcendental Meditation

In the next few chapters, I'll be going into some detail about the Transcendental Meditation Program. Although TM has been a life-changer for me, I realize that with the subtitle of this book, *Gurus and Psychics and Shrinks, Oh My,* you may be less interested in reading about silent meditation and mantras and more interested in embarking on some of the crazier adventures in the captivating depths of the warped psyche. If that's the case, skip to the chapter, *The Occult.* That should fry your circuits and deliver some Blair Witch Project-level thrills. From that chapter on, I don't let up on the wild ride. You can always come back to the TM chapters.

If you're fine with easing into the crazy with a measured step, stay here and continue with the chapters in order. Here's the TM story:

Our little four-room apartment on Hampstead Heath, 8a Elm Row, NW3, was the picture of charm, despite being not big enough to swing a cat. It occupied the ground-floor of a large house on a cobblestone walkway that led down to art shops, a pub and a small community theater. The neighboring houses were all at least two-hundred years old. We often spent evenings walking on the heath among the soft meadows and abundant wildflowers, old-growth trees and rare fresh air in a city plagued by smog. I loved living in Hampstead and still miss it to this day.

One evening, as we left an Indian restaurant on the Hampstead High Street, I noticed a poster in a store window with a picture of Maharishi Mahesh Yogi. I remembered him as the Indian guru made famous by his relationship with The Beatles and The Beach Boys. The poster announced a lecture on Transcendental Meditation. It stirred my memory of seeing my ex-girlfriend, Sarah, sitting as still as a cast iron lawn ornament on the floor of my 38th St. apartment... allegedly doing this thing called meditation. Upon seeing this poster, my interest reawakened, and this time I didn't have the excuse that the teaching center was all the way across the country. Here, it was less than a block away. I did my best to remember what Sarah told me about the practice and related it to Maggie. She said without hesitation, "Let's give it a go!"

Fast forward one week. The lecture took place in a quaint little Quaker building called Friends Meeting House. I don't remember much from that evening, other than two people dressed like bank managers gave the talk. I found this odd. With the subject at hand, I would have expected them to look more like hippies on the way to a Grateful Dead concert. Nonetheless, I was captivated by what they described. Because Maharishi was a Hindu monk, they made a point of assuring us TM was not a religious practice. I didn't care. This looked like an opportunity to get a taste of what my Hindu book described, without having to erect a statue of Ganesh on my front lawn. We liked what we heard enough to sign up for the course.

They told us they'd be teaching the following Saturday through Tuesday. A couple of odd requirements caught my eye, though. First, they required us to be drug free (the recreational chemical kind, not your asthma inhaler). No problem. A month prior, I was at a party smoking some weed, and my friend, Rob Gordon, arrived, having spent a few days on a TM residence course. I offered him a joint, and he scowled, "Are you kidding? I wouldn't put that shit in my body if you paid me."

Aside from the verbal wet blanket, I must admit he had a point. I put the joint out and never picked up another to this day.

Requirement number two — bring a clean new handkerchief, some flowers and some ripe fruit. While this seemed a little odd, it also felt kind of Indian and folksy, so we happily went along with it.

By now you've probably figured out I'm telling this story from the perspective of a newbie, which I was at the time. Later, I became a TM teacher myself, so of course I learned how to do all that I describe below.

It's now Saturday, and I show up at the designated time and location that turns out to be a suburban house in North London, again folksy and down home. No complaints. A woman named Margaret meets me at the door.

"You're Mr. Ryan, I presume," she says with a delightful Queen Elizabeth accent.

"I'm Margaret Hall. (We shake hands) Please come in. We'll be going up to the second floor for your instruction."

She escorts me upstairs into a room with two chairs and a white sheet covered altar. On the altar is an array of hardware comprising a brass tray, a brass incense holder, an item that looked like a tiny Aladdin's lamp, a small brass pitcher of water and a framed image of an older, bearded gentleman in orange robes sitting on a large carved chair. Though I'm here and committed to doing this, I again sense religion creeping in.

Margaret smiles and says, "I assure you, this is not a religious ceremony and you are not being inducted into a Hindu sect."

I am relieved that I did not see a pitcher of Kool Aid on the altar.

"I will perform a brief ceremony, and you may simply observe."

At some point, someone told me this helped keep her ego in check. Not sure why she thought she needed to address her ego, but what do I know?

I'm still holding on to my odd little offering of fruit, flowers, and handkerchief, which she now takes from me, placing the fruit and handkerchief on the side of the altar. She then takes my flowers, pulls one out, and hands it to me, asking me to stand and watch. With that, she breaks into a quaint little song in a language I later learned is Sanskrit. It's a pleasant tune, and while she sings, she performs some synchronized actions, like laying the handkerchief on the tray for one verse, the fruit during another, lighting the little lantern and waving it in a burning circle around the picture. Same with the incense, which is now burning and smelling wonderful. Finally, she places her flowers on the tray, invites me to do the same, kneels before the altar, bowing down to the painted portrait, then turns and smiles at me. I'm not sure why or what I'm supposed to do, so I just stand there while the *priestess does her stuff. She motions for us to sit down and says something about not sharing what she is about to tell me. Then she repeats a strange word a few times. She also asks me to repeat it, but I can't understand the word. I ask her to spell it. She does, and I follow her instructions about how to use my new word.*

I won't go into much more detail, because you know, "don't share," but she left me to do the silent repetition of this word, or mantra, as she called it, for about ten minutes, and I loved it. When I finished, I experienced a pleasant buzz, all happy and peaceful. I'll be damned if this TM thing doesn't work! Sarah nailed it. My loony lady from San Francisco, in all her chaotic shenanigans, was on to something.

TM Teacher Training

Maggie and I took this TM thing pretty seriously. After practicing the technique for about a month, we signed up for what they called a Weekend Residence Course at Keele University in Staffordshire, England. Over a two-and-a-half-day weekend, we would learn some yoga asanas, do multiple meditations, and learn more about consciousness. This was exactly what I wanted — non-religious, self-development with a spiritual twist, ironically being taught (over video) by a Hindu monk, Maharishi Mahesh Yogi.

During the course, I learned about cosmic consciousness. The second I heard the word, my ears perked up. Affectionately nicknamed CC, it is said to be a mental state in which the mind and heart are free from worry and strife and filled with bliss. One becomes a witness to activity, rather than the doer or victim, responsible for neither prosperity nor adversity. Our instructor, a smart, funny guy named Rick, presented CC as the ultimate freedom from the clutches of the insatiable ego. Damn! That's what I'd been looking for since those miserable teenage years. I learned later that CC is more of a stepping stone and is not a mental state, as described. It is the first stage of recognizing our true identity.

I wouldn't describe the course as a chill weekend in the country. It was more like taking a college level course in consciousness. We didn't come for intellectual stimulation; we came for R&R. I sometimes closed my eyes and zoned out during the lectures, and that made the two days feel restful and easy… except when a bull from a neighboring farm tried to gore us while we were on a walk. Here's the story:

After our Saturday lunch break on a beautiful English spring afternoon, Maggie and I take a stroll down a path not far from the university. Having walked about a half mile from the campus, we hear a rumble and feel a thumping on the ground beneath our feet. To our shock, we spot a bull bearing down on us, full throttle, about two hundred feet away and closing in fast. With pounding hearts and visions of disemboweled matadors, we pick up the pace away from him, trying not to act scared and run, which might further encourage him to deliver us to the afterlife. We soon learn his intentions are doomed from the start. Along the side of the path, strung between evenly spaced four-foot poles, are thin rows of wire, creating what appears to be a laughably frail fence separating his meadow from our path. Not very encouraging.

To our surprise and relief, and prior to shared cardiac arrests, at the last second, he violently hits the brakes just short of the wire, skidding to a dust cloud finish and releasing a loud, angry, and disgruntled snort. Then I notice the reason for his abrupt aborting of the mission. The wire is fastened to the posts by glass insulators. It's an electric fence! Big Angus had probably tested it a time or two, and was not interested in repeating the experiment. Seeing stars and having your brain scrambled by 20,000 volts is rarely enjoyed by animals or humans.

We are greatly relieved. Fan our noses, do we. Flare and snort his nostrils, does he. Back to Keele trot we.

As for the course, we did a bunch of meditation and learned about consciousness from some scientists who put TM to the test in the lab. Their results were impressive. From my side, beyond the science, it just made me feel good. It was also nice to see the lab results demonstrating that the positive effects weren't all in my head. And that was it. The course ended early Sunday afternoon, and we made our way back to London.

This was the beginning of our making a deep commitment to the TM movement. After about six months of regular meditation, we were totally hooked. We signed up for an evening course called "The Science of Creative Intelligence." I expected an average-Joe-friendly, light foray into what makes us smart or dumb. Again, we were presented with a university level curriculum on consciousness, brain functions, and a bewildering array of very abstract concepts regarding alternate cognitive functioning. I'm not complaining. It was deep and fascinating… just not what I thought it would be.

But beyond the intellectual experience, in our lives, we seemed to have entered a new personal phase. Whether work or play, our interface with the world had become more relaxed. Worries were less frequent, sleep switched from restless to restful, maybe sex improved, not sure about that one, but we both experienced an overall improvement in wellbeing.

After a year of meditation practice, I became curious and wanted to know how and why TM worked. I assumed if I became a TM teacher, I'd learn everything there was to know on the subject.

I said to Maggie, twisting her arm a little, "Are you interested in taking a TM teacher training course with me? We'd have to drop everything we're doing and disappear for six months. They don't teach it in London. It's an in- residence course at a beautiful Elizabethan mansion called Royden Hall in the South of England."

I sold it like we'd be enjoying a long vacation on the French Riviera. She had been an antique dealer, but that business demanded too much time and effort for too little profit. After a few years of retail drudgery and exhaustion, she gave up, cut her losses, and closed the shop. To fill the financial gap, she now worked part time as a barmaid, pulling pints at the local pub.

With a grin, she said, "Hmm… I don't know… oh sure, let's do it. I could use a new career."

My risks were a little higher, though. I wasn't a part-time service employee. I enjoyed a solid, full-time career. Leaving town for six months might have a substantial downside. It could open up a space for another guitarist to glom my gigs, leaving me the proverbial choice of waiting tables or driving a cab.

Nevertheless, my enthusiasm trumped my fear, and maybe trumped my common sense. Without regard for the possibility of this being a dumbass misstep, I declared, "Screw it, let's do it."

Subsequently, we signed up for the six-month, in- residence Teacher Training Course. In the next few weeks, we closed out our apartment lease, put our furniture in storage, paid any outstanding bills and set out for this potential career-crashing adventure in consciousness — the TM Teacher Training Course.

I said to Maggie, "What are we doing? Are we nuts?"

She replied, "Yes," as we hopped in the car and began the ninety-minute drive to the course facility, Royden Hall, East Peckham, England, where we would sequester ourselves with thirty other TMers and learn all about consciousness and how to teach TM. We would hunker down, do hours and hours of meditation, high-level courses, lectures and instruction and eventually become the next lot of initiators or better known to outsiders as teachers of the TM Technique.

So, what was this course like? Our schedule comprised rounding, lectures, meals, and watching videotapes of Maharishi, as well as experts in the field we studied that day. Rounding consisted of a set of yoga asanas, a breathing exercise called pranayama, then a period of meditation. We would perform several rounds each day, one set when we awoke in the morning and another at around 4 PM. Videotaped lectures were shown in the morning, afternoon and evening after dinner. Our day ended with ten minutes of a taped series of Vedic chants collectively called the Samaveda.

Most of the day was pretty routine. Not so much the rounding. While I enjoyed the yoga asanas (simple yoga postures to keep the body limber, stretch out the muscles and tendons and get the blood flowing), pranayama, and twenty minutes of meditation, the rinse and repeat factor could become intense quickly. We'd do three rounds in the morning before breakfast, and three rounds in the afternoon. For me, these sessions weren't simply relaxing, nor were they meant to be. They were mental forays into cosmic realms that I had only dreamed existed. After a couple of rounds, I would start to "transcend" or go beyond normal consciousness, feel incredible bliss as the superficial "I" in me seemed to step back from normal experience, revealing a greatly expanded entity unto itself, and a deep sense of bliss would set in. Thoughts would drift in and out, but were rarely the focus at these times. This bigger "I" appeared to be the true "me" while the mental hash appeared to be just noise. It was amusing to notice that this noise was my usual mental state, the part of my being that I erroneously considered to be the real me on an average day.

These experiences taught me otherwise. To be clear, this wasn't every meditation. Just as often, I would zone out, enjoying memories like the time in my college years when I went swimming with friends in the Atlantic in February after running down a snow-covered beach (I may or may not have been under the influence of adult beverages at the time), or the practical applications of Einstein's theory of relativity. Also, pondering the dinner menu could fill an entire meditation. Sometimes you just get temporarily lost on the road to enlightenment.

There is another byproduct of rounding that can be not so pleasant. We call it, "unstressing." TM has the potential to get rid of stress, anxiety, tension, and trauma. That's the good news. The bad news is sometimes when the process is taking out the mental garbage, the emotional pain of the original stressor rears its ugly head and can feel almost as bad as when it was acquired. Most often, you'll have no idea what stress is being eliminated, only the resultant pain. It happens rarely and not enough to make you want to hit the brakes, though. The bliss at most other times makes it worth a few bummers now and then.

An important part of the curriculum involved exploring the seven states of consciousness, waking, dreaming, deep sleep, Transcendental Consciousness, Cosmic Consciousness, God Consciousness, Unity Consciousness, and the bonus eighth one, Brahman Consciousness. There are entire books exploring this subject and a wealth of info on Google, so I won't expand much on it beyond saying the levels starting with Cosmic Consciousness are a big deal. Though we were led to believe that in a few short years, we could achieve these higher states, I know of only a tiny handful of people that have done so, and several of them were not practicing TM. Don't get me wrong, though. The practice is well worth it, with or without the achievement of higher states of consciousness.

The course became routine after a short while, and we settled in. With our regular schedule and decent food, it was just a matter of learning the curriculum and passing the exams. No big deal… until the last two weeks. The final learning responsibility in becoming a TM teacher — memorize "The Steps," the final instructions for how to teach someone to meditate. This series of lessons arrived via two suited gents who reminded me of Tommy Lee Jones and Will Smith in *Men in Black*. They spoke softly but did not pull their punches when making clear how we would conduct ourselves from this day forward, and the big one, what we would wear. Here's what almost got me a ticket home without a diploma:

"So... from this day forward, you will always conduct yourselves with dignity. Your language will be refined, and your demeanor will be pleasant."

(Low key, quiet mumble and grumble from the class).

"Remember, you represent Maharishi and the TM Movement, and all eyes will be on you, judging your behavior, day in and day out."

(No response, just serious expressions like we were joining the CIA and were about to get read in on some international threat).

"Women will wear conservative dresses, or skirts with blouse and sweater, subtle jewelry and minimal makeup."

(Quiet reluctant agreement from the women).

"Men will wear suits and ties at all times."

This is where I step off the wagon. I'm a musician. I WILL NOT wear a suit and tie while playing at an outdoor summer festival, or club, or anywhere unless I'm teaching TM. I ask the wiseguy question:

"So, you're saying that even at the beach, the men have to wear a suit and tie?"

I've heard some unhinged tow-the-line responses to odd questions, but this one took the cake -

"Yes."

"You're kidding, right?"

"No, I am not. You represent Maharishi and the movement, and you'll wear a suit at all times."

There was no humor in his response, and frankly, no common sense. The President of the United States wouldn't wear a suit and tie at the beach. My solution was simple. I ignored him. I'm happy to wear the proper attire when I'm teaching. When I'm off duty, I'm off duty, and I wear what I like. All the men on our course agreed. We also agreed that such an impractical directive probably did not come from Maharishi. There were a number of power abuses going on in the movement in those days, and from time to time it felt like the gestapo.

As I said earlier, it wasn't that I was so keen on becoming a TM teacher. I just wanted to learn how it worked. I taught a few people after I graduated, but before I did, I went on a US tour with a popular singer. She forbade me to wear a suit and tie.

Most of the stories of our days at Royden Hall are not all that interesting… but why not hit one of the more… spicy ones? During that time, I had a sharp mind and an excellent memory. As part of our training, we were required to memorize a procedure called "The Checking Notes." This is a question and repair inquiry to help meditators straighten out any problems they might have meditating. I was one of the first to memorize the twenty pages of notes, so I received the inglorious appointment of testing other students. There was a bit of tone from some of my older classmates whose memory wasn't so sharp when I tested them, but any animosity was short-lived.

Meanwhile, an attractive young Scandinavian woman named Eva, on another course at Royden, caught my eye. Because we only had one cafeteria, students in all classes took their meals together. One evening at dinner, Eva sat across from me at the next table, and our eyes met. She caught me off guard and it threw me. I was there with Maggie (not yet married, mind you) and this Scandinavian beauty was smiling and staring me down from the next table. Ok, yes, I flirted a bit, but it didn't go beyond a wink and a smile.

A week later, our instructor pulled me aside and said, "There's a woman on the other course that needs her meditation checked. Would you be willing to check her?"

"Of course," I replied. "Who is she?"

"Eva, the Scandinavian lady."

"Ohhhhh shiiiiit," I say to myself. "Ok, you can do this. Be a good boy and get the job done, no hanky panky." Here's the story:

I walk over to the next building where she's housed, climb the stairs to the second floor, check room numbers and find her door.

"Knock, knock,"

(The door opens, and she looks surprised at first and begins to smile).

"Hi! To what do I owe the pleasure of your presence at my door?" Or something flirty like that. I was pretty flustered, and lord, she was smoking hot.

"Um, er, I was told you needed your meditation checked, and I took the opportunity to help you with it," I said in a shy voice.

"Well, that's very nice of you. Please come in!"

After some brief small talk, she sits up on her bed. I sit across from her in a chair and begin the checking procedure. I ask a few standard questions, note her answers, and slowly guide her into

62

meditation. After a short time, following the procedure, we bring the student out of meditation and ask them if it was easy. I did, and she responded, "No, not really."

We go through the procedure again, I bring her out after a few minutes and ask, "It was easy?"

"I'm sorry, no."

It's my job to figure out what's going on, so I ask with a smile, "What is the problem?"

"I can't relax."

"No? And why is that?"

She detonates the nuke. "Because I'm so attracted to you."

My heart almost pops out of my chest. She is sitting cross-legged in a skirt on her bed, without regard to what's on display. She is smiling, her playful blue eyes are inviting, and in that moment, I have to decide. Eva has made it clear she is mine for the taking, but I'm there in an official capacity, and her boyfriend (did I mention she had a boyfriend?) is in the next room. Maggie is in the main building, unaware of what's going on. I'm dying, but I just can't do it. The idea of a teacher seducing a student is mega verboten, and if I am to maintain any integrity, leave alone risk being ratted out by her boyfriend, who would be livid if he found out, I had to toe the line. The instructions from the checking notes for any "can't do" situation involuntarily leave my lips.

"Even with this attraction, we can still have thoughts. If we can think, we can repeat the mantra as easily as any other thought."

That's what I tell her, the official response from the checking notes, but what she hears is, "Sorry

63

babe, I'm not that attracted to you. Now let's try that mantra again and get this over with before we're late for dinner."

The sexual tension couldn't have been killed faster if someone set off the ceiling sprinklers. I watch in misery as her beautiful smile turns into a pout, and the moment is blown away like an empty trashcan in a hurricane. I have rejected her, and Eva, in all her voluptuous Scandinavian beauty, is not used to being turned down. She is not happy.

"Oh... ok. Wow..."

We finish the procedure with her agreeing that her meditation is now fine, and though she is polite, her words upon my getting up to leave could be translated to mean, "Don't let the door smack you in the ass on the way out." And that was my first experience as a fledgling teacher of the Transcendental Meditation Technique.

TM Under the Microscope

So far, I've praised TM for all its benefits. That is not the entire picture. Let me begin by saying that if anyone tells you self-development is easy and painless, walk away. Yes, TM is a simple, painless technique that has a marvelous ability to resolve *some* issues. Can it resolve *all* issues as I've sometimes heard around the movement? Maybe, over several lifetimes! But some vasanas (behavioral tendencies or karmic imprints from the past which influence the present behavior of a person) are as stubborn as a bloodstain on a white sheet. I can tell you from the experience of having practiced meditation for fifty years, I still suffer from a few less-than-ideal behavioral tendencies, the sources of which I have yet to uncover that hurl me into reactivity with the right trigger. To loosely quote Ram Das, "There is nothing quite like family to jettison your experience of enlightenment."

The TM movement went through a difficult period a few years back when I was told it was infiltrated by the CIA. The agency was allegedly suspicious when the movement declared itself as the "World Government of the Age of Enlightenment," giving out titles to TM Teachers like "Governors" and movement leaders as "Rajas," the literal meaning being "kings." Meditators were "citizens" and those who had taken the TM Siddhi course were called "Citizen Siddhas." When Maharishi discovered this incursion, he expelled the agents with the warning to report exactly what they had seen without exaggeration and declare that the movement had neither desire nor intention to rule or take over the USA or the world. It is a government that encourages growth in consciousness to aid in avoiding war, international hostilities, crime, and the negative tendencies of the troublemaking ego. That's a pretty lofty goal by any measure. With the relatively small number of people practicing the technique, the goal remains on the wishlist. They need to get their numbers way up to turn their vision into a reality.

Before I go deeper into the global effects of the TM program, I'd like to introduce and describe the TM Siddhis. In 1977, Maharishi Mahesh Yogi came on the Merv Griffin show and introduced the TM Siddhi program. The Yoga Sutras of Patanjali, an ancient text on obscure yogic practices, had been misunderstood and superficially translated as almost folklore in the past. Maharishi, with a deep understanding and grasp of Vedic culture and the Sanskrit language, re-translated them and discovered that practicing certain "sutras" in a mental technique taught over several weeks, could have a very beneficial effect on both the practitioner and those in their immediate environment. One controversial siddhi being taught is "yogic flying." Yes, levitation. I am a veteran TM Siddha with forty-five years' experience. Have I levitated? Nope. Have I seen anyone else levitate? Nope. We hop around on mattresses, but staying up in the air on a hop? Nope. Again, I cannot stress enough that enlightenment, supernatural powers of yogis, and all the stories surrounding these phenomena are a big deal. Those who master any of it are extraordinary human beings. I don't mean to dishearten the faithful, but I know of no one who has mastered the TM Siddhis and only a tiny handful of those who have attained spiritual enlightenment. One possible reason is that we don't live in a vacuum. We are all deeply affected by those around us and world circumstances. For practitioners to be able to make the siddhis do what they are purported to do, the world needs to calm down quite a bit. An example given by a movement leader is the following: "You may have clear 20/20 vision, but if you are standing in the midst of a pea soup fog, you will not be able to see the building across the street."

TM, or any meditation technique, for that matter, is valuable for many reasons above and beyond the extraordinary claims. The benefits are well worth even an inconsistent practice. It is exhaustively documented that TM can help with blood pressure, anxiety, depression and many maladies. But in saying this, I want to manage expectations. While the TM Siddhis enhance the results of meditation, the odds are against your attaining the ability to make yourself invisible, walk through walls, travel to different universes, or fly like a bird, much as I wish they weren't. The siddhis do make you feel pretty good most of the time though.

So, beyond personal experience, what is the global effect of group meditation? Control studies proved that one percent of a population in a specific radius practicing TM would lower the crime rate in that population. Statistics, borne out by police records validate this claim. With individuals practicing the TM Siddhi program, the number needed to produce the reduced crime effect was considerably less. They calculated the number to be the square root of one percent.

To prove this, in June 1993, siddhas, or practitioners of this technique, were invited to take up residence in a hotel in Washington, DC for two months and practice their TM Siddhi program. The effect of the gathering of siddhas in this way was called Super Radiance. Movement statisticians predicted that the violent crime rate over June & July would drop by around 20%. Police officials laughed it off as absurd, but were happy to provide statistics to prove the TM movement wrong. In fact, the crime rate dropped 23.3% exceeding all expectations. After going through the data rigorously, they concluded that nothing else going on at the time could have created such an unprecedented drop in crime. Along with the reduction in violent crime, the following results were tabulated:

- President Clinton experienced improved approval ratings ($p = 5.29 \times 10^{-8}$).
- Media positivity toward Clinton showed a net change increase ($p = .01$).
- Emergency psychiatric calls decreased ($p = .009$).
- Hospital trauma cases decreased ($p = .02$).
- Complaints against the police decreased ($p = .01$).
- Accidental deaths decreased ($p = .05$).
- Quality of life index improved ($p = 3.22 \times 10^{-5}$).
- When the group left at the end of July, the crime rate climbed up again.

I will add that I attended this event, and it was a blast. I reconnected with friends from all over the world that I had met in my travels. And as one might expect, meditating with thousands of like-minded people had a very profound effect on our minds and bodies. We enjoyed an all-around wonderful experience.

I give high kudos to TM and the TM Movement's accomplishments. Their heart is in the right place, and I have genuinely benefitted from the practice. I maintain a few small gripes about how the organization operates, but I suspect the problems TM faces as an organization are similar to most movements. There are power struggles, a sometimes-military self-righteous attitude among the mid-level managers, and a tendency to be a bit starry-eyed about flying and superpowers. But most people never come into contact with this echelon, and the issues are not deal breakers. I salute the current movement leaders at the top, Dr. John Hagelin and Dr. Tony Nader. Both are brilliant scientists, sincere, honest people and excellent leaders. I highly recommend the TM technique as a self-development tool. The organization provides substantial lifetime support once you learn the technique and a wealth of advanced programs for those wishing to dig deeper into the realm of meditation and consciousness. If this sounds like something you might benefit from, I say go for it. I did. No regrets.

The Occult

In 1974, after learning TM, I became fascinated with anything Eastern and mystical. The Hindu book of my teens may have been the initial stimulus, but though I never became a Hindu, my interest in mysticism and the occult continued burgeoning after TM. I devoured books like, *Many Lifetimes,* by Joan Grant, *Psychic Self-Defense*, by Dion Fortune, *A New Model of the Universe*, by P. D. Ouspensky, Colin Wilson's *The Occult*, *The Yoga Sutras*, by Patanjali, *Autobiography of a Yogi*, by Paramahansa Yogananda, and many others. Egyptology and pyramids fascinated me to the point where I built a wooden, one-foot-square-base model of the Great Pyramid of Giza to see if placing butter one third up under the apex would preserve it. It did. It also caused the crystals on the edge of a razor blade to realign and sharpen as predicted. That's my recollection and I'm sticking to it.

It was the influence of TM which led me to these alternative studies. Though the TM movement avoided associations with anything non-mainstream science, in England, there existed a powerful undercurrent of beliefs among meditators about miraculous achievements of yogis and a strong interest in alternative philosophies and mysticism. Westerners tended to be suspicious of these studies and preferred to adhere to what they learned in houses of worship. Not so with us meditating buzz heads. No, we didn't quite wear tinfoil helmets, but we also didn't reject phantasmal ideas that seemed reasonable based on our flashy experiences in meditation.

I mentioned the occult above, and I'll now describe why I weaned myself away from occult studies. In a word, fear. Dion Fortune goes into great detail on how to ward off evil spirits in her book on psychic self-defense. Colin Wilson wrote a vast 800-page tome on the occult, and I read every word. Whether his or her analyses on the subject proved accurate, they could be disturbing for those who endured teachings about evil spirits and demons from kindergarten through college, i.e., me. I will relate one life experience that will illustrate why I ended my exploration into this often-disturbing subject. From my journal:

While living in London, Maggie and I were close friends with a couple who we shall call Jack and Debbie. Jack was an enthusiastic proponent of white magic (The use of supernatural powers for selfless purposes). He studied it, understood it, and practiced it as a hobby. One afternoon, Maggie and I dropped in on Jack and Debbie, and there was something strange about their apartment. It was quite cold. I asked Jack if he had turned down the heat, and he assured me he had not.

"You feel it too?"

"Yes. What's going on?"

He said earlier that day a musician acquaintance, troubled by off-and-on bouts of heroin addiction, had visited them. A short time into the visit, in a strange outburst of joy, his friend exclaimed,

"Wow, I don't know what just happened, but I feel great. I feel better than I've felt in years."

With that, his friend declared he was going for a run in the park and left them wondering what happened. That's when the apartment began to feel chilly. While Debbie and Maggie chatted, Jack and I checked the thermostat — locked at 73°. We put our hands near the radiators — all cranking out heat, and still... the four of us experienced a distinct chill. Though it could have been my imagination, the room seemed distorted, longer than I remembered and somehow not quite solid, changing as I moved around. The experience matched my first attempt at wearing progressive lenses — you turn your head and the room warps in the peripheral vision. I was wearing contact lenses though, not progressives. The experience defied reason.

Jack had a theory based on his occult studies. According to ancient Hebrew texts, there are dark spirits known as qlippoths. These spirits or entities sometimes seek out and attach themselves to drug addicts whose immune systems and aura have been weakened from their drug habits. As the legend goes, qlippoths thrive off the addict's low vibration drug-fueled energy. While the idea of vampire spirits of Hebrew antiquity seemed far-fetched to me, I could not deny the very physical chill in the room and the almost nightmarish dimensional warp I was perceiving. Jack elaborated:

"Debbie and I have been meditating in this room for a couple of years, and the energy we've created and infused in the apartment is quite pure. My theory is our ambient light energy triggered a separation between the qlippoth and our friend, and now it's

here in the room absorbing the higher vibration and much greater abundance of energy. Hence, our friend experienced a tremendous relief upon the disconnect, and we're experiencing the cooling effect of the vacuum the entity is creating with its actions and presence."

In my mind, I declared bullshit. Though I was interested in the occult, this explanation seemed a bridge too far. The thought that we were experiencing, first-hand, the presence of a disembodied evil entity seemed ridiculous and, at the same time, quite disturbing. My first thought was, what're we gonna do? Call Ghost Busters?

No need — Jack was a ghost buster. He had studied exorcism rituals and was as knowledgeable as any medieval priest. However, he had never performed one. Lots of knowledge; zero experience. What could go wrong?

His plan was to wait it out and see if the entity (if there was one) left of its own accord, or take matters into his own hands and perform a formal exorcism. Maggie and I wanted no part of this insanity, so reaching for the door handle while wishing Jack and Debbie a pleasant evening, we got our butts the hell out of there, leaving Jack to deal with his Opus Dei rendition of The Haunting of Hill House!

Though we talked about it at length on the way home, by the end of the evening, Maggie and I had written the whole thing off to Jack's quite vivid imagination. After watching an episode of Monty Python's Flying Circus on the BBC, we turned in for the night, switching the lights off at around 11:00 PM.

To our dismay, the peaceful night did not remain so. A frightening disturbance shook us out of a deep sleep at around 3:00 AM. The sound of howling wind outside and the wailing of several cats had us sitting bolt-upright in bed, wide-eyed and white-knuckled, wondering what the hell was going on. Gale force winds were rare in London, and we were unaware of any outdoor cats living in the neighborhood. Translation: two people spooked to the point of wanting to get dressed, jump in the car and GTF out of town as quickly as possible. Too stunned to do anything, we just sat up in bed staring out the window at the trees, leaves, and loose paper getting blown around by this raging weather phenomenon and waited it out. The storm took about a half hour to die down, and eventually we calmed down enough to go back to sleep. Upon awakening the next morning, and to minimize the fear factor, we wrote the storm off to an unusual weather anomaly and feral cats we had not noticed until last night. Animals are often ferreted out of their hiding places by unusual weather, no? Convinced that an innocuous rationalization was preferable to exploring the possibility of a supernatural event, we inserted our ostrich heads into our imaginary sand holes and got on with the day.

After a delicious Sunday morning breakfast of pancakes, eggs, coffee and OJ, we decided to check in on Jack and Debbie to see how they were doing in their little Transylvanian hovel. When we arrived at their apartment, I noticed it felt warm and comfortable. The room dimensions had also stabilized. But I noticed Debbie looked white as a sheet, and bug-eyed like she had seen a ghost. What Jack then told us made our blood run cold.

Apparently, the chilly feeling in the apartment did not let up after we left, so Jack took matters into his own hands. They had smooth oak floors in their apartment, so they pulled back the rug and chalked out a large white circle. Jack described the scenario:

"I marked the North, South, East & West points on the circle, and Debbie and I sat down on a couple of pillows inside it. The circle is supposed to protect us from dark spirits who might want to jump in when the exorcism gets going. Once everything was in place, I began reading the prescribed words from the book of exorcisms I found at the occult bookstore in Camden Town. The idea was to conjure the archangels, Michael, Gabriel, Uriel, and Azrael into the circle, then ask them to cast out the dark spirt and toss him back into whatever dimension spawned him (or her). I kept saying the words of the exorcism prayer, over and over, and that's when things got crazy. First, a lightbulb from the ceiling fixture popped out of its socket and exploded on the floor next to Debbie, who let out an ear-piercing shriek. It scared the crap out of me because, unlike the bulbs you yanks have, our light bulbs don't unscrew. They're locked in bayonet fixtures. You have to push 'em in and give 'em a quarter turn counter-clockwise to release the tabs from their slots. Then they slip out. They do not just fall out. Ever.

"This was the bugger's attempt at breaking my concentration. I wasn't having it, but I admit, I almost wet my pants. The qlippoth just wouldn't go, so I tried harder to focus, repeating the archangel chant, over and over. Debbie was freaking out, but I

had to ignore her or this vibe sucking psycho beast from hell would become our permanent flat mate.

Maggie and I are glancing at each other like, "Is he playing us?" Jack notices and says,

"Wait. It gets worse. Kitchen and dresser drawers started opening and closing, rattling and slamming. Silverware crashed down onto the kitchen floor. Dishes shook on the shelves like they were possessed. Another light popped out of a table lamp and exploded a few feet away. Now we're both fucking losing it, but I continue the chant, like a stuck record. We did not agree to be flat mates with a heat-sucking qlippoth in a virtual refrigerator.

"After about thirty minutes and Debbie getting ready to jump out the second-story window, everything suddenly stopped. The room went silent and began to warm up. After a few long minutes of quiet and a survey of the mess of silverware, drawers and broken glass strewn all over the room, we declared, yes! It was over. We won! Algol, the patron demon of addiction and broken light bulbs, had given up and pissed off. The archangels prevailed, the exorcism worked, and everything went back to as normal as could be expected with our living room looking like a WWII bombsite in East London."

It was now understandable why Debbie looked so pale and freaked out. She did not speak other than a faint hello when we arrived at the apartment. She just sat, curled up on the sofa wrapped in a blanket, staring wide-eyed into the middle distance. Jack, having vanquished the unseen evil entity, looked like a knight who had just slain Fófnir! He was upbeat and eager to talk about the night for as long as we wanted to listen. It didn't help Debbie's PTSD when I related our experience of the howling wind and screaming cats we had experienced in the night. Everyone felt a little shudder upon the revelation that our mini cyclone occurred at the same time as the drawers, dishes and lightbulbs were flying around the room at Jack and Debbie's house — 3:00 AM!

Though I was not there in that apartment with them, Jack was not prone to hyperbole, and Debbie was not displaying complete shock in a vacuum. Whether or not Jack exaggerated the tale, something very disturbing had happened that afternoon, evening and night, in both their apartment and outside ours, and I will never forget it as long as I live.

From that day forward, I vowed to stay rooted in studies and practices that keep things psychologically balanced and within this dimension, and my life has been the better for it. One exception. You may read about it in the following chapter.

The Oracle of New Rochelle

Because of my experience with the insane exorcism from the previous chapter, dabbling in psychic inquiry was no longer on my bucket list. Only in a masochistic moment would I read a few chapters from Bram Stoker's Dracula and go to bed looking forward to eight hours of nightmares. My only other first-hand experience with the psychic realm was consulting a storefront gypsy. To her credit, she was quite skilled in the art of telling fauxtunes (phony fortunes) with a Walmart crystal ball. Nothing she said about my past was true. Nothing she predicted about my future came true. Nice lady, but not someone whose counsel I would rely on... bless her heart.

But then things changed. My friend, Dr. Susan Plunket, a clinical psychologist, had been wrestling with many of the same life questions as me, and in her research, discovered an internationally acclaimed psychic, Vincent Ragone. She described a session with him that was so mind-blowing, it gave me chills. She also mentioned that he was a consultant to the Pentagon and four presidents, carrying the highest level of security clearance. It was a safe bet he couldn't snake-oil that many VIPs without ending up in a military tiny house, so I thought I'd give him a try. She wrote his number on a yellow sticky, handed it to me, and with cautious enthusiasm, I gave him a call... or should I say calls, the number of which practically put me on a first-name basis with his answering service. When he eventually returned my call, the only appointments he could offer were a year and a half out. I had no idea what I was doing a week and a half out, so I picked a random date and booked the session. Time passed, the day finally arrived, and here's the amazing story:

It's May 9, 1979. My appointment with Vincent Ragone is today. What seemed like a cool idea a year and a half ago, had me feeling quite apprehensive now. I mean, who knows what will shake out, conferring with this high-level liaison to the spirit world?

I don't keep a car in the city, so the Metro North train is the transport of choice. Vincent lives in New Rochelle, NY, and I live on 38th St. between Park and Madison in New York City. Grand Central Station is only a short walk from my apartment, so I hike the four blocks up Park Avenue, enter the station and purchase my ticket. But something weird is going on. My relentless mental narrator is urging me to retreat. Damn! What's up with this resistance? Here are the top five thoughts my mental DJ has on rotation:

1) Go home. Idiot!

2) He will suck the soul out of your body.

3) This is dumb. You're dumb.

4) Weren't you supposed to pick up your laundry today?

5) "Driving that train, high on cocaine...."

I do my best not to listen despite the catchy Grateful Dead tune.

The trains come every thirty minutes, so the wait isn't long. Nonetheless, I keep glancing at my watch as my doubts continue their annoying assault. The 12:18 rolls up. Doors open with a whoosh. People rush out, some smiling, some frowning, some holding hands with their kids, some holding briefcases, all trotting up the stairs to their meetings, lunches and adventures amidst the architectural canyons of NYC. I'll bet none of them are going to see psychics.

When the crowd clears, I board the train, find a window seat, the doors close, and we slowly begin our journey north. I'm not a seasoned commuter with a good book. I'm a hot mess, with a vivid imagination, squirming in my seat as we slowly make our way up to Hogwarts.

The views coming out of NYC on Metro North are not memorable. We lumber through Harlem, rolling along the tracks between hundreds of tenements and high-rise apartment buildings, then eventually we speed up a bit, but only for a few minutes. I feel the brakes kick in as we begin making all the mind-numbing routine stops — Melrose, Tremont, Fordham, Botanical Garden, Williams Bridge, Woodlawn, Mt. Vernon East, Pelham, and finally... New Rochelle! Thanks to my annoyingly active imagination about what's on the docket, it is the longest thirty-minute train ride I've ever experienced.

Ok, I'm here, but it's 12:50 PM. My appointment isn't until 1:30. "What to do?" I say to myself as I stand on the platform. "I am not showing up early! No sir. Nobody likes people who show up early, and do I really want to annoy a psychic? I don't think so."

I take out my mental calculator — "Vincent's home is about a ten-minute walk from the station, so let's grab a newspaper, find a bench and we'll kill a half hour." (We being me and my always-on, fucking mental narrator)

After the thirty-minute, self-imposed paranoia-fest, I toss the unread paper in the nearby trash can, and following the written directions, start my slow walk to God knows what.

Arriving ten minutes later, I ring his doorbell, fully expecting to meet the equivalent of Lord Voldemort. Within a few seconds, a very ordinary man comes to the door, and to my great surprise, greets me with a smile and offers a warm handshake. Vincent Ragone looks to be in his late forties, slim build, glasses, greying temples, khakis, plaid shirt, and unthreatening. I guess I can dial down the paranoia a few notches.

He invites me in, and as I enter the vestibule, he asks me to remove my shoes. I oblige, then follow him to his study, where he takes his seat on a dark brown leather armchair and invites me to make myself comfortable on the couch opposite him. To start some light conversation, I tell him I arrived in New Rochelle early but didn't want to disturb him if he was in session. With a smile, he says,

"You have a good sense of intuition, James. Why not use it? If you had, you'd have known my morning was free and that I could have taken you early."

"Use my intuition?" I thought. That's a first! I was brought up to follow a list of rules and procedures, and intuition was not on that list. I imagine it might have been on the mortal sin list, along with seeing psychics. I'm starting to like this guy. The whole interaction seems so calm and normal.

But normal ends quickly, and the weirdness begins. Vincent asks me for my glasses. Keeping my WTF thoughts to myself, I pass them over to him and he explains,

"Glasses, or articles of clothing that we wear frequently, absorb our vibratory essence and are used by psychics as tools to tune in to each client's long history."

A moment passes while he handles my specs, running his fingers slowly along the arms and gently pinching the lenses several times. I sit, quietly staring at nothing in particular, because without my glasses I see nothing but a colorful blur of undefined objects.

Handing them back to me, he says, "I will now connect with my physician on the other side, and he will assist me with your comprehensive physical examination."

"Other side?" Goosebumps... I'm reminded of my occult readings and not in a good way. And what's with this "comprehensive physical examination" thing? That wasn't on the menu. With little choice in the matter, I play along.

Vincent says in a quiet, pensive voice, "One moment... ahh, there he is."

To myself, "Oh man, there who is? Bloody hell."

He explains, "The good doctor does not suffer the limits of clunky modern technology. As he is in spirit form, he can enter your body and examine it in ways that no incarnate doctor or medical device can. Patients have found his diagnoses to be 95% accurate. Let's give him a moment to do his examination..."

I nod ok with my eye on the door. A minute or so passes...

Vincent seems to speak to the open room like he's on a phone call with a headset, "Very well... yes... I understand."

"The doctor tells me you have an anomaly with your coccyx (tail bone). Let me look into this... yes... you had an accident when you were six. You were coming down the basement stairs, slipped and fell halfway into a metal barrel. One leg went into the barrel, the other landed on the basement floor. As a result, you slammed your coccyx into the edge of the barrel, bending it three degrees to the left side. This injury has pinched some nerves and limited the circulation to your feet. He suggests you see a chiropractor and have an X-ray taken to determine the appropriate treatment. Once the coccyx is straightened, the circulation will return to your feet.

Dear reader, you must understand that not only have I never told anyone about falling on the barrel, I have not had a single thought about it since it happened. It hurt like hell, but it was a bruise from a misstep like any other a six-year-old might experience during childhood, so no big deal. My mom, in her usual hyper manner, screamed, yanked my pants down, examined what was basically some redness and a bruise, saw that I could still walk, decided nothing was broken, and let it go, as did I. But once Vincent mentioned it, I remembered it like it happened last week, and he diagnosed this condition with the help of a discarnate doctor, living on *the other side!* Make no mistake, we're talking about actively communicating in real-time with a physician in the afterworld.

Upon reading this, my doubting cousin, Dr. Barbara Larkin, who helped me with the editing of this book said he must have a research team looking up whatever they can find on his clients so he can pretend he has these extraordinary powers. I reminded her, "That shit wouldn't fly in the Oval Office or the Situation Room, where he spent a lot of quality time over several decades. No internet in those days either." She agreed.

When I got home, I called my mom and asked,

"Do you remember an accident I had when we lived in Livonia, where I fell down the basement stairs and landed straddling dad's waste barrel?"

"Yes, now that you mention it. That was so long ago, but I do remember it. You were crying so hard, it frightened me. You seemed to be ok though, no broken bones as I recall."

"Has anyone contacted you asking questions about me?"

"No, why?"

"Never mind, long story. Gotta go. Bye!"

Mom didn't take me to a doctor, so no medical record of it exists. I submit that this was an extraordinary diagnosis, with no easily explainable methodology. This dude possessed some potent psychic chops.

Let me describe the aftermath. On a friend's recommendation, I made an appointment with a chiropractor, Dr. Jonathan Bard DC. When I arrived in Dr. Bard's office several days later, I warned him, this wouldn't be an ordinary visit, that I had a weird story to tell. He said he loved weird stories and to let it fly. Upon describing my session with Vincent, Dr. Bard seemed skeptical, but confessed he had heard weirder stories. He booked me for an X-ray session the following morning, after which we met again. As I entered his office, his wide-eyed expression was a mix of astonishment and incredulity.

"Who the hell is this guy you went to see?"

"Why? Was his diagnosis bullshit?

"No! Look! (Showing me the X-ray) He was 100% accurate! Did he take an X-ray? No, wait, why would he do that? How did he even know there was a problem? Did you tell him about your chronic cold feet? Is he a doctor?

"Uhhh... no, he's not a doctor, he didn't take an X-ray, and no, I didn't complain about poor circulation in my feet. As a matter of fact, I've never complained to any doctor about cold feet, so there is no medical record of the condition anywhere but in my head. I just assumed some people have poor circulation at their extremities. I've lived with it all my life. He just handled my glasses for a few moments, made a psychic call to a doctor in the spirit world who did the exam and gave him the report. I know. The story sounds insane. I sound insane, but I swear that's what happened."

Dr. Bard acknowledged the psychic doctor approach was a first for him, but regardless of his skepticism, the diagnosis was spot-on. We began treatment once a week, and in about a month, the coccyx was realigned and the circulation returned. My feet are now warm as toast under all but the most extreme cold conditions. Sometimes they are too warm and I have to go barefoot to cool them off. No complaints!

After this astonishing experience, I thought, "Wouldn't it be fun to go before the Harvard Medical School review board and present this new diagnostic technique — ask the patient for their glasses, smudge the lenses with your sweaty fingers, call or text an available dead doctor, ask him to enter the body of the patient, remembering to request that he or she not take possession of their soul, and…" Continuing with the session:

Vincent says, "Ahh… you believe as I do in reincarnation. (Yes, I do, but I hadn't mentioned it.) Dear me, what is it with you and the Catholic priesthood? I see you have been a priest in several lifetimes and narrowly escaped being one this time around."

I never mentioned anything about even being a Catholic, leave alone my early desire to be a priest. No one knows about that except my parents and Sister Francis Xavier, my sixth-grade teacher at St. Cletus elementary school in La Grange, IL. Vincent conjured that up from who knows where, and now this is becoming quite remarkable. I continue listening in wide-eyed wonder.

"Your choice of guitar as your principal instrument is an excellent step in your evolution as a musician."

I never mentioned I was a musician or played the guitar.

"In a previous lifetime in India, you played tabla. You have an excellent sense of rhythm as a result, and now combining your seasoned timing sense with melody has made you quite an in-demand musician… am I correct?"

"Yes, I suppose so. Please continue."

He smiles, "...and another lifetime as a traveling minstrel in Italy during the Renaissance... much previous musical education...all the more reason to continue your musical journey in this lifetime!"

Vincent seems other-worldly, communicating with his eyes closed and speaking with a strange, high-pitched voice in an unusual sing-song cadence. His tone is oddly formal for two dudes just sitting in a home office chatting. Despite his weird communication style, I'm starting to have fun, especially since we're now talking about my favorite subject, music!

"Dear me, more religion, more religion," he exclaims, shaking his head dubiously. "Another incarnation in the service of your religious beliefs. You were a traveling sadhu, also in India several hundred years ago. Your spiritual journey has spanned many lifetimes, James. (Calling me by my formal name). You have turned your back on the world many times in pursuit of enlightenment, only to come up short at each life's conclusion. Such a pity. Perhaps your lesson now is to learn that on earth, spiritual pursuit must include the body, not ignore it, starve it, and treat it like it's a burden. Does that make sense?"

I nodded yes. Though I practice meditation, I live in the material world and am quite happy to enjoy all it offers. At the same time, I try to keep my nose clean. Medium success on that account. Exercise and yoga are also a regular part of my routine, so we'll put checks in those boxes.

Vincent concluded his mild criticism of my pursuit of spiritual matters with a warning, "Beware of gurus." Before I could ask him why, he was on to the next subject. "Your wife, Maggie, I believe her name is..."

I never mentioned I was married, leave alone her name. I suppose he could have noticed my wedding ring and took a wild guess, but the ring wouldn't be flashing "Married to Maggie," would it?

He goes on to acknowledge our marital problems. Though I hadn't mentioned we were struggling to keep our marriage afloat, he is right again! I feel some relief when my new favorite psychic assures me, we would have a long and happy marriage.

Vincent got the long marriage part somewhat right. Maggie and I were together for fourteen years, but the happy part? Not for a while. I'll give him an 80% on that one, but with a caveat. Predictions can be self-fulfilling. After asking him some very personal questions about my future, he told me psychics will never reveal a client's date or time of death. He said with squinting eyes and a knowing grin, "What crazy antics might we get into if we knew we had another thirty years to live?"

Psychics also avoid making predictions about painful events on the horizon if nothing can be done to avoid them. Failed marriages come into that category, and if he told me Maggie and I were destined for failure, I might have pushed the divorce date up and left her before the time was right, i.e., the time to meet the "correct" second wife. I put correct in quotes, as that marriage also failed. I can only assume it was correct because it taught both of us some lessons about ego, control, and empathy.

Upon not telling me my date of demise, he declared that our time was up. No problem from my side. I was ready to bring this wild ride to an end. So, with deep gratitude, I bid the Oracle of New Rochelle farewell.

Vincent Ragone left this world on March 8, 2011. Beyond a funeral notice with one kind comment, I could find no records of his existence, save a few comments in other's stories, always with high praise. I would love to include more about him personally, his exploits, his pentagon sessions, etc., but those records are either classified, sealed or don't exist. Dr. Susan, who gave me his number, told me that Vincent was an extraordinarily private person, and it is unlikely that there is any documented personal information about him. She included the possibility that Vincent Ragone might not even be his real name. Cue Twilight Zone theme.

Tai Chi

After practicing TM for about eight months, my friend Jim, a fellow meditator told me of a wonderful system for toning up, relaxing and self-defense. He called it Tai Chi and related the following story:

An elderly Tai Chi master tells his students he is going for his morning walk in the forest. One of them says,

"Master, would you like us to accompany you... for your safety?"

The master smiles and says, "I'll be fine. Tend to your chores, and I'll be back within the hour."

When the hour is up, and their master has not emerged from the forest, the students begin to worry. A few of them set out to see if he is ok. About ten minutes into the forest, they discover two pairs of tracks. One bears the imprint of their master's sandals, but to their shock, the other bears the imprint of a tiger. Now with deep concern, they continue along the path, stepping quietly and cautiously to make as little disturbance as possible. But there are birds chirping all around them as well as all the usual forest sounds. This is strange. When tigers are stalking, the sounds in the immediate area of the forest quiet down, sometimes even becoming silent. Has the chase come to a deadly end? Is their master dead?

As they approach a clearing, what they see shocks them. Their master is sitting on the ground cross-legged, meditating. A few feet away lies a dead tiger. From the angle of its head, it appears its neck is broken. Within a short time, their master opens his eyes and gazes at them with a look of compassion and love.

"Did I not tell you I would be fine? Sadly, our beautiful friend here mistook me for prey. Let us gather in silence to bless his soul so he may travel safely to the afterworld and dwell in peace among his ancestors."

While there is no obvious moral to the story other than trust your Tai Chi master when he says he'll be ok, what stands out is the power of this incredible martial art. Of course, this is just a fable, but its principles are rock-solid. Tai Chi is the art of using your opponent's violent energy against them without aggression.

In the above story, it is told that at the last instant after the tiger leapt and was in mid-air, jaws wide open ready to close on the master's head, the master moved a few inches to one side, grabbing the tiger's lower jaw. The tiger's body continued its airborne trajectory, but the jaw stayed put in the Master's iron grip. The confused tiger felt the agony of its jaw being dislocated and lowered its head to relieve the pain. Its weight, forward momentum, and confusion brought the tiger down on its head and broke its neck. Of course, there was great strength on the master's part from years of training, but the key was timing, efficiency of movement, and the element of surprise. He used the tiger's overconfidence and momentum to bring its life to an end.

When Jim said there was a Tai Chi master giving classes not far from us in London, my curiosity got the best of me. As I mentioned in an earlier chapter, I was skinny and not athletic in my youth and was often bullied. Those memories left some mental scars and at least a little ambition to learn how to defend myself. As an adult, though, no one had ever attacked or bullied me. The urge to learn how to defend myself was more like a quiet curiosity borne of childhood trauma. I would sometimes think, "What if I could kick like Jean-Claude Van Damme or Chuck Norris?" Over the next year, I learned to do just that.

I will refer to our practice in the following story as both Tai Chi and Kung Fu, though they are not quite the same. Kung Fu translates loosely as "meritorious work." It can apply to artists, fighters, chefs, or anyone who has developed extraordinary skill. Tai Chi is an inner martial art, a form of meditative movement. Our prospective teacher, Master Liu, taught both. The slow movement was to train and memorize actions that in a fight would be performed at lightning speed, i.e. Tai Chi becomes Kung Fu.

The four of us, Jim, his wife Celie, Maggie, and I, took the London underground to Master Hsu Chi Liu's dojo and signed up. While I didn't want to start a new life of bar fights and bone breaking, I loved the idea of getting fit and mastering a martial art.

At the beginning, things were fine. The signup was uncomplicated — we agreed to an insurance waver saying any injuries were our own responsibility and agreed to attend all classes for a given period. They also required us to purchase a training uniform — loose-fitting beige yoga pants and a black collarless shirt/jacket to be worn in all classes.

Master Liu was a diminutive figure, about five foot five, with a thin handlebar mustache and a full head of hair. I'd say he was in his late forties. He spoke in a booming voice and rarely smiled. He also wasted no time in establishing military order. I had envisioned cheerful people in the park going through slow motion movements, leaning out with one leg forward, arms sweeping through the air, in blissful communion with their bodies and nature.

Not in this dojo. Our lessons took place in the upstairs of what appeared to be a small, disused factory. There was no heat, and the floor was covered in mats lined with straw, not foam. If you hit the mat hard, you might not break a bone, but you'd add the color purple to the limb or head that made the unfortunate contact. In the winter, we had to wear sweaters under our thin cotton jackets or freeze. We were always barefoot. Socks were forbidden, so our feet never got warm, and I never got used to any of this. I hated it. Why did I continue? I made a commitment, and the hopeful end seemed to justify the miserable means, at least in the first few months.

Master Liu had an assistant named Beth, a London woman who resembled Hilary Swank. Since I like Hilary, the comparison only goes to appearance, not likability. Beth would take over the lesson after Master Liu would show us the movement du jour. As we executed the motions, she would shout and berate us. We were new, a little clumsy, and had no idea WTF we were doing, yet Beth treated us like we should have known the

93

current movement before they even taught us. To her, she had a class full of slackers, not students. Instead of encouragement, she treated us to a constant barrage of insults, and a rare "That's better." We felt like inmates in a federal prison.

At one point, I tore my yoga pants and had to replace them. Fiona, the woman attending the dojo shop, was a heavyset, tattooed Scot from Glasgow with an evil temper — not a person I would mess with. She had a swagger and a way of holding herself that suggested if you said the wrong thing, she would hop over the counter, thrust her steel fingers through your ribcage and rip your heart out, stuffing it down your throat, still beating.

Upon my request to replace my ripped pants, Fiona shouts me down for my ineptness and suggests I might not qualify for a replacement.

"Why don't you just sew it, you clumsy idiot?"

"Seriously? That's where you want to go with this?"

No, I did not say that. You know, the extracted bloody heart thing...

Instead, I tell her, "Because I don't know how to sew. You wouldn't like the result."

I have a delightful vision. I imagine her struggling in quicksand up to her neck, begging for help and me saying to her,

"Why don't you just climb out?"

So clever, the things we think of to say or do after the fact.

There are other students waiting on line, so with a huff, she tosses the new pants on the counter, takes my money and moves on to the next student. The dojo entrance is right behind me, and the temptation to bolt is overwhelming. I don't. Instead, I suck it up, head to the locker room, put on my Tai Chi outfit, and climb the stairs to the next class. I'm a "commidiot." (committed idiot) None of us are quitters, and we want this situation to work. We treat it like the equivalent of Camp Lejeune, training for the marines. That works for us in the short term.

With the help of Frau Beth, Master Liu taught us movements and routines that resembled what I had seen in the park, but their maniacal attention to detail set them apart from anyone teaching the meditative form. They demanded micro-accurate movement and balance. There was nothing loose or slack about anyone or anything in this military dojo.

The beginning of the breakdown came during lectures. Master Liu would spend hours teaching us about Shaolin monks and Kung Fu, putting down every other system of martial art, meditation, and the I Ching. He insisted his view was the gospel. Odd, because he taught Chinese history at the local college. I can't imagine they'd let him get away with such a negative, one-sided spin on every study and opinion but his. In our lessons, his favorite expression, injected after the description of other systems such as those practiced by TV and movie martial artists like Bruce Lee, was, "They are idiots! Frauds! They do not practice Kung Fu!"

Sometimes his rants were persuasive. Always, his rants were tiresome. Psychology teaches that directing derogatory remarks and constant criticism towards others reflects deep insecurity. Criticism is a ruse to cover up one's own feelings of inadequacy.

Still, we continued, keeping our commitment to remain under his tutelage for the semester.

It wasn't all bad, though. We enjoyed a lot of the adventure, despite the awful personalities of our instructors. Maggie and I used to practice at home in our little Hampstead apartment. We worked well as sparring partners. If one of us forgot a move, the other usually remembered it:

One evening, after a good practice session, our musician friend Barney came by to pay a visit. Barney is six-feet-six, slim and fit, and asks, "What's with the uniforms? You guys going to a cosplay party?" We tell him of our little Kung Fu adventure, and though he listens patiently, he has his doubts about how effective it would be for five-foot-three Maggie against a man of his size. With a smile and a wink at me, she stands up and challenges him.

"Barney, would you like a demonstration?"

He reluctantly agrees.

"Come at me like you're going to grab me and try something naughty."

"Oh, come on. I'm twice your size. You don't have a chance."

"We'll see. Do it!"

Barney shrugs his shoulders and lunges for her. The next thing he knows, he's on his back on the living room rug. Maggie nailed the move. It was very basic stuff, but she had practiced it so many times, it was second nature.

Barney looks astounded. I extend a hand to help him up. He accepts and says to Maggie, "Well, that was impressive! And you learned that in the last few months?"

"Yes. I've never had to use it, and I hope I never will, but yes, that is the kind of thing they teach."

I confess that I too am impressed. Maggie isn't a tiny woman, but she is also not an Amazon or anything close.

She learned to use Barney's momentum and the trick of moving out of the way at the very last instant while holding on to a specific part of his body. It caused him to tumble and crumble. She was kind enough to not break his neck.

I don't believe I have ever been more fit than during that time. Like the fable of the master and the tiger, great strength is required to perform Tai Chi in its true martial form. With a brutal amount of exercise, I learned to do multiple one-armed pushups on my fingertips. My balance on one leg became unshakable. My self-confidence had grown, and my insecurities about defending myself had all but vanished… and that's when the trouble began.

After learning the basic routines, Master Liu introduced us to the martial factor. Martial means characteristic of or befitting a warrior… not a Sunday in the Park with George poser. We weren't just waving our hands in the air like hippies at Woodstock … We were vanquishing imaginary aggressors, breaking imaginary arms, legs, ribs and necks. Our hands were becoming lethal weapons, ramming imaginary nose bones into imaginary brains to kill our imaginary opponents instantly.

Showtime:

Master Liu asks for a volunteer during some matches we were performing to get used to using the routines and movements in a fight.

I step forward, eager to please, but soon realize he wants me to attack him. I'm six feet tall, he's five-feet-five. Like Barney, the idiot in me thinks this is a pushover, a silly mismatch. Though I'm a lowly student, I'm bigger, packing quite a lot of hard-earned strength, and I outweigh him by thirty pounds.

To everybody's surprise, he says,

"Strike me in the face with all your might."

"Seriously? No. Please. I can't."

"Full force, all you've got. Stop acting like a little girl."

"Ok, you asked for it."

With no further thought, I take an aggressive stance, feet anchored to the floor, hands in a ready-to-strike Jackie Chan pose and launch my right fist towards his face with all my weight behind it.

To this day, I do not know what happened or how. I only know my fist never reached his face. When I regained my wits, I found myself face down on the mat with what felt like the front wheel of a Chevy Blazer pressing into the middle of my back, and my arm bent at an unnatural angle in intense pain.

With a calm voice and a faint smile on his un-smacked face, Master Liu says,

"That is Tai Chi! That is what we are doing here. You are not flailing your arms and doing an ignorant dance. You are defeating an aggressor without mercy. If necessary, you are ending their life."

Sweet Jesus, this is not what I signed up for. Get in shape? Check. Get a little discipline into my life?

Check. Learn how to kill people with my bare hands?
UNCHECK!!

Soon after that episode, we all left the dojo of Master
Hsu Chi Liu for the last time. We did not clock out,
and we did not ask for permission, nor did we consult
Beth, Master Liu, or Fiona, the mega-bitch in the
dojo shop. We just walked out the door into the cool
evening London air and brought this chapter of our
lives to an end.

Though I no longer studied Tai Chi, I continued
practicing the routines for a while to stay in shape. I
mentioned earlier, violence and bullying faded with
my entry into adulthood. But that changed once I
became competent in Tai Chi. Occasionally, I
experienced random jerks coming up to me and
picking fights at clubs. I'm a musician, so I paid my
dues gigging in these dives but never experienced
aggression like this in my adult life before Tai Chi.
Something in my presence betrayed that I was a
fighter. It was as if I was a violence magnet, walking
around with a sign on my back, "Attack Me!"
Brawling never had a place in my life, and I wasn't
about to let it start now. With every incursion, I
chose the first principal of martial arts — talk the
aggressor down. Violence is always the last resort,
because it could end in serious injury or death. I had
been taught how to kill with my bare hands. If
pressed to decide between forfeiting my life or
neutralizing a drunken jerk trying to kill me, I would
take the proverbial tiger by the jaw and use his
momentum to end his life. This mentality didn't
work for me and the odds favored it ending badly if
I continued.

Once I realized my new aura of military confidence was threatening my life far worse than being an average peaceful citizen, I stopped my Tai Chi practice, and there were no more attacks. I went back to being a musician, making people happy instead of cracking their skulls.

I included this story, because Tai Chi is in every way, self-development. The question is, what part of the self are you developing? If you practice it with a group of friendly people in a positive environment, it is a meditative activity that promotes strength, balance and a sense of physical well-being. I highly recommend it. Just try to avoid the Paris Island version that has been the subject of many B Kung Fu movies.

So, time to grade the product. Is the martial form of Tai Chi a useful modern-day practice? Yes, for physical fitness, but in America, where guns are ubiquitous, of what use are hand to hand combat skills? Master Liu did not teach us how to dodge or catch bullets in our teeth.

In my first book, I told a story of how a Mr. Clean lookalike named Skipper used to give karate demonstrations at a NY City club called Steve Paul's Scene. I'll give you the recap here as it is pertinent to the current subject:

One Saturday evening, two young Brooklyn thugs came into The Scene and approached Steve Paul, demanding regular payments for protection and a piece of the club's profits. Steve told them to take a walk. They returned the following night in greater numbers and started beating up customers and trashing the club. Skipper, the black belt karate expert and bouncer, jumped into action, testing his skills in a real-life skirmish. With arms and fists flying, executing lightning punches, and high-kicks, he launched a few ruffians into the air and had them smacking into the brick walls. Skipper at least slowed down the action. But unbeknownst to him, one of them had snuck up behind, and with a swift crack, smashed a large glass ashtray on the back of his head. Skipper hit the deck like a sack of potatoes, and with that, our hero was out of the game. The thugs destroyed what was left of the club, and without mafia insurance or enough personal funds to make the substantial repairs, Steve Paul's Scene closed forever. It was not like the martial arts movies where one master knocks out fifteen villains. It was real life, and it was a real-life fail.

Here is my impression of martial arts these days. Maybe for some they are useful in defending against a mugging, and maybe they're a good idea for women to defend themselves against abusers and rapists. They're also a great idea for Keanu Reeves and Jason Statham to train for their ultra-violent action movies. But for guys like me, who have experienced violence seeking me out and following me like a shadow for no logical reason other than my Tai Chi practice, I'm done. Gambling my life for my watch and a few bucks in my wallet makes no sense to me.

EST

Do you remember EST (Erhard Seminars Training), that breakthrough, transformational self-development forum that thrived during the years 1971 through 1984? If not, here's a description. In the most simplistic terms, EST was a lecture and experience-based two-weekend, sixty-hour program designed to help people take responsibility for their lives, to be truthful and present in their personal and business interactions and own their faults, rather than blame them on others. Werner Erhard, the founder of EST (birth name, John Rosenberg), a deep thinker and striking figure, described Zen Buddhism and the teachings of Allan Watts as the foundations on which EST was based. The training was popular in the US during its time, enrolling nearly half a million enthusiastic trainees. While most found it a valuable undertaking, some developed an EST personality, acting obnoxiously self-assured and treating friends and family like they were not ok if they didn't sign up. We referred to them as EST-holes. There are volumes written about Erhard and the evolution of EST and his subsequent seminars, so I'll leave that to you, dear reader, to Google if you're interested. But for the sake of this chapter, I prefer to share *my* experience with EST rather than a lengthy description from a brochure. The year is 1982...

Basic Training

Here's a description of my first day on the EST Basic Training Course. Hard to forget that day!

We are gathered in a large meeting room in a hotel in New York City. There are about two-hundred of us seated, listening as a "trainer" gives a lecture on an aspect of integrity. It's not very interesting. A young woman gets up and excuses herself over and over as she slides her way across the shifting knees of people sitting in her row, sidestepping her way to the aisle. The trainer stops his lecture and shouts out from the dais in a booming voice:

"You! Lady heading for the aisle. Where are you going?"

In a shy, embarrassed voice, she responds, "Sorry, I didn't mean to disrupt the class. I need to use the bathroom."

"Go back to your seat."

"Excuse me??"

"Go back to your seat and sit down."

"I... I... need to use the lady's room!"

"What was the agreement you made before starting this training?"

"I... I... don't remember anything specific. What are you talking about?"

"Somebody please remind our forgetful friend about the bathroom agreement."

A few hands go up. A middle-aged man shouts out,

"No one may use the bathroom outside of breaks, no exceptions!"

The trainer shouts, "Correct. Do you remember making that agreement?"

"I don't know... Whatever. I need to go."

"Tomorrow, skip that second cup of coffee. Now go sit down."

"You can't be serious!! OMG!"

"Does anyone detect a humorous tone in my voice?"

He looks around the room. Silence. Some dread. The woman, looking dejected, angry and a tad desperate, sidesteps back to her seat and thumps down with an irritated huff, glaring at the trainer and crossing her legs like a vice grip. An expression of anxiety and pain replace her glare.

This happened only once in the first weekend, never again in the remainder of the training. Does it seem unreasonable? To some, yes, and perhaps enough of a reason to avoid EST at all costs. But is there a point to this seeming tyranny? I believe so. A primary tenet of the training was to teach people to keep their agreements. If one wants respect from friends, family and colleagues, their word must be dependable and sacred. We all signed a list of agreements prior to entering the training. Unfortunately, the bathroom agreement was buried in an innocuous list on several pages of the course description and requirements. The average person might not even notice it, leave alone take it seriously. It's unlikely this woman even read the agreement. But the trainers treated every item like an oath.

Everyone hated this part of the program. It was infamous and well-known among self-development junkies. I cheated — an EST graduate friend warned me about that little clause, so I avoided any liquid at breakfast.

EST took the same position about being on time. If you made the mistake of coming in late, you were required to stand up and get dressed down in front of the class. Why? Because you signed an agreement to abide by the ground rules, and in the checklist was your agreement to show up on time. Once we realized the futility of defending a broken promise, no one was late for the rest of the training.

Here's an example of the non-tyrannical, educational side of the program. In a brilliant episode on day two, our trainer blurted out the following:

"Let's talk about victimhood. Who here is a victim? Who has been victimized? I want to hear your story. Please stand up and share your story with the group."

Many hands go up, and the trainer points to a woman in the fifth row. The woman slowly begins a shocking story of abuse that happened when she was thirteen. By the end of her story, she is sobbing. With neither acknowledgment nor sympathetic comment, the trainer moves on. In his booming voice, he asks,

"Who else has a victim story?"

With a sad, quizzical expression, the woman sits down, not quite certain why neither she nor her story received any further attention. Our trainer calls on a man a few rows behind the now sobbing woman. The man relates a story of how an apprentice made a critical wiring mistake on a commercial electric jobsite that almost electrocuted him. He shows the burn scars on his hands.

"Anyone else?"

The man, also perplexed by the absence of comment or sympathy, reluctantly sits down.

Another sexual abuse story ensues from a nineteen-year-old woman.

No comment.

"Who else? I want to hear more victim stories. Let's get them out in the open."

An older woman stands up and tells a horrific story about her almost fatal accident, but something strange happens in the room — there's a faint snicker from someone towards the back. A few people are grinning but trying to hide it, certain their reaction is grossly inappropriate.

The trainer interrupts the current speaker.

"What the hell is going on?" Dead silence. The thoughtless snickering ingrates are now holding their breath for fear of being called out and humiliated in front of the group for their apparent schadenfreude.

"Do you think this is funny? People are spilling their guts out and some of you are laughing? What the fuck is the matter with you?"

A long pause ensues, as many are trying to contain their inappropriate reactions. It's almost like when someone farts in church. No one wants to be caught laughing, but like the fart, it's almost impossible to hold in.

To everyone's shock and surprise, the trainer is now displaying a slight grin.

In a quieter voice, he asks, "What happened here? The room morphed from horror to humor by the fifth story. Why?"

Silence. People are no longer smiling. No one has a clue. But everyone is laser-focused on the trainer, waiting on the edge of their seats, because they know something unexpected and probably profound is about to be revealed.

"Some of you started to laugh, because the idea of tragedy-laden victimhood seemed to lose its energy after the fifth story. You went from shock to subdued chuckling in under ten minutes. Why?"

Not a peep.

"You may not be ready for this, but bear with me. There is NO SUCH THING AS A VICTIM."

Gasps from the audience.

"I'll repeat that. There. Is. No. Such. Thing. As. A. Victim."

Grumbles ensue. A muffled "bullshit" from the back. Here it comes:

"I can see most of you are resisting this with every fiber of your being, but let's look deeper. There is a lead-up to every tragedy. There are decisions we make, one by one, that lead to our being in a certain place and time that can cause a tragedy. Sometimes those decisions are unconscious and innocent.

Take for example a woman who decides to walk home by herself after a party, because she lives in what she believes to be a safe neighborhood. Perhaps the woman notices a sketchy guy was staring at her all night with a less than healthy expression. In this hypothetical scenario, she might ignore him and the obvious red flag. She leaves the party. He follows her as she walks home alone, attacks her, and the rest is history. Was this her fault? Not if you look at it from a victim's point of view, but if you step back, you can see the decisions she made leading up to the tragedy. She disregarded the creep that was staring at her and chose to walk home alone. She chose to believe her neighborhood was safe. While you may feel she had every right to make those assumptions, life often teaches us that an assumption is often the first step toward a disaster. Did the electrician examine the apprentice's work before he touched the contacts? Did he assume the apprentice knew what he was doing? Yes, he did, and paid the price.

Perhaps this is a heartless and unfair way to look at situations like rape or plane crashes, and in an ideal world, you would be right. But we don't live in an ideal world. Wake up and pay attention to your surroundings, people, or accept the consequences!"

This trainer was now pissing off a lot of people, including me. Many disagreed with this declaration of non-existent victimhood, but he shot their arguments down, one by one, with impeccable logic. It's hard to imagine justifying a victim's personal responsibility in situations like rape, i.e. the "blame the victim" perspective often taken by defense attorneys so prevalent in our warped society today. But the logic of tracing back all the steps leading up to a problem, regardless of whether they were stupid, innocent, or just unconscious, made sense to me. It wouldn't help the current crisis, but it might help prevent the next, and that was what he was getting at — to wake people up from their unconscious, sleepwalking stupor and pay attention to their lives, their surroundings, their actions and the actions of others to avoid calamity. EST encouraged people to practice present moment awareness and get the hell out of their daydreaming heads. It was a lesson I cherish and a lesson that went a long way towards jettisoning any remnants of self-pity to which I still clung. Blame is a powerless position. Yes, in my mind, I could exonerate myself by blaming others, especially my parents, for my personal tragedies and feel some relief, but blame was putting others in charge of my life. That's not ok.

There was a great deal more to this training than what I've mentioned, but again, I'm not here as an EST advocate. I'm giving you a few salient examples of what I experienced. I also remember little more than what I've told you, so there's that! Also, as I have mentioned a few times, I'm a musician, not a psychologist, so I'm feeding you a generous portion of *my* opinions based on *my* experiences. I encourage you to examine your own lives as I have done. Your opinions may differ, but taking the blinders off and living a conscious, present life will be an enormous improvement over the passive, daydreaming lives that so many of us live. The EST terminology for present moment awareness is "living at cause." "Living at effect" describes blamers and complainers — how so many of us live our lives.

So, being a long-term TM meditator and an advocate of "TM: the solution to all problems," why would I want to enroll in a controversial mind exploration forum like EST? Because Maggie and I had entered a difficult period in our marriage, we needed answers to why we were such a confrontational mess. The TM movement doesn't provide counseling, and the time frame for meditation to solve all problems is not one week or one year… or maybe not even one lifetime, despite its ability to make you feel better quickly. We didn't have time to wait. EST looked like a reasonable solution to help us root out the problems that were threatening our relationship. EST brought them to the forefront for us to deal with. It didn't erase them, though. That was up to us.

I experienced some transformation after this unusual forum. My energy was up, and I had a positive outlook for the future. Unfortunately, I also picked up some of the jargon from the training and got some snarks from friends and family about being too slick and a know-it-all. I didn't quite get the EST-hole walk of shame from anyone, but there was some pressure to talk like a normal person. I relented.

EST was a step in the right direction, but you notice it's not the last chapter in the book. For one thing, I wasn't finished with the journey, and another, the benefits wore off after about six months. Taking additional EST "advanced" courses in serial succession was of no interest to me. Catching my breath and trying to integrate what I'd learned was, so in the absence of trainer mania, the "getting it" factor faded. But I was not prepared to stop my search. My quest for the holy grail of sanity continued for many years after this.

We're not quite done with EST, though. The next chapter will give you the ins, outs and nail bites of the advanced EST program known as the Six-Day Course. If you have a fear of heights, this one will get your heart thumping. If you have a fear of sex, this one will also get your heart thumping. Same, if you have no fear of it.

The Six-Day Course

Did I like everything about the EST training? No, not everything. Upon graduating, the debriefing team strongly encouraged us to sign up for the continuing education programs being offered by the company. In the previous chapter, I said I wasn't willing to do that. A couple of exceptions stood out, though, so I broke my own rule. I allowed my arm to be twisted and signed up for one of them.

The course comprised weekly seminars that lasted about three hours per evening. I enjoyed the first hour and a half where we explored some fascinating subjects and ideas. Then came the recruitment. The second half of our meetings involved an hour and a half of mind-numbing, super-aggressive enrollment speak.

"How many people did YOU bring this week?"

"Do you not value what you got out of your two weekends with us?"

"Are you not willing to change people's lives? Do you not have the guts?"

"Where is your courage?"

"Does changing the world mean nothing to you?"

"Who will commit to bringing two people next week?"

"I don't see your hand up. What's your problem?"

"How many people will you bring next week?"

I thought this was a onetime anomaly restricted to the first evening of the course. I was so wrong. Every single class followed the same format: 50% class, 50% recruitment. We all hated this. The organization knew that and didn't care. This is how they survived — recruit and engage an unpaid sales team, and bank the profits. I didn't last long, dumping the course after three weeks of this nonsense.

But I did not dump EST. I still felt there was value to be gained by sticking around, and another course they offered caught my attention. It was called the Six-Day Course, a series of challenging subjects or modules, covered in great detail over six days, and held upstate New York, in residence. It sounded intriguing, and I couldn't resist. I love residence courses. Maggie and I signed up the following week. Little did we realize it would be a round trip to hell. Why the hyperbolic descriptor? Because there were moments where the pressure was so intense, it felt like hell, but there were also some days that were exhilarating. I'll try to present a balanced review. Let's start in the general category, sleep. I doubt if I had one day in six where I got more than three hours' sleep. Here are the broad strokes.

Part 1: Ropes

We start early in the morning and rarely finish before 3 AM. Once we sail past midnight, we are provided with two-foot-long logs. If you are falling asleep, you stand up, go to the outside aisle and pick up a log, holding it over your head or on your shoulder. The physical strain of supporting a log does wake you up, at least temporarily, but what amazes me is how the trainers can go on and on lecturing for hours and not need a log themselves. So annoying.

An important side-function of the six-day course was health improvement, and weight adjustment was at the top of the list.

After lunch on the first day, a woman in a team T-shirt steps up to the podium in the front of the cafeteria, picks up the microphone, and speaking in a cheery camp counselor voice, says, "Good afternoon, and welcome to the six-day course!! How's everybody doing??!!"

A few half-hearted "Goods" and "OKs" from us, still with food in our mouths. She shouts,

"GREAT!!"

Then she runs through all the ground rules, the dos and don'ts for the week. With the laundry list and mandatories out of the way, she lowers her voice and says in a more serious tone,

"Some of you are slightly overweight. Some are quite overweight. No one is obese, but anyone who is overweight to any degree, please check in at the table in the back of the room to get your special meal pass."

Maggie nudges me with a less than subtle finger to my ribs,

"Go on. Get back there."

True, I had a slight gut from spending more time in the recording studio and less time running 5Ks, but really? The two sticks of celery and water table?

"Fine," I grumble as I get up, join the walk of shame and shuffle my slightly overweight butt to the back table to be given my culinary Scarlett Letter. Now we can add hunger to sleep deprivation.

To be fair, the food isn't terrible. They just cut back on the quantity and offer no desserts or sugar. There's that hell.

Also included in our health program is a run to increase stamina. Every morning before our diminutive, joy-free breakfast, we are required to run a 1K up a mountain trail. When I say mountain trail, I mean jumping over fallen branches, tree stumps, ruts, ditches, rocks, and often uphill. For me, this is insane. Sure, I used to run around the playground in my early years and play soccer and baseball as a teen, but those days ended when I became a musician. I am strong from lifting amplifiers and keyboards, but let's not confuse strength with stamina. My stamina is in the toilet, and I don't need an uphill 1K to remind me. It's helpful that the staff is ever-present on the trail cheering us on. But how many times can you hear, "Come on, you can do it!" before you want to scream bloody murder and strangle someone? I'm thirty-something, huffing and puffing, heart pounding, sweating and doing my best to hold up the rear with the septuagenarians, and I vow to never again let myself get into such a state of physical shitness. But in this moment, I have no choice but to make it to the finish line, running, walking or crawling, every single fucking morning.

Regarding the various modules, note-taking proved irrelevant. The course was not linear. There were lectures, but it wasn't the detail of the talks that mattered. It was the overall message. Because the lectures were often combined with physical activities and group discussions, I decided to just soak it all up and hope I'd leave with some intrinsic value and an improved sense of well-being, maybe even a touch of self-realization. We were encouraged to embrace anything we saw, heard or experienced that moved us towards higher awareness.

That's the overview. I'll now tell the stories that have remained in my memory, some fond, some foul, hopefully, all worth your time if you ever decide to take a journey like this.

The course began with us lining up and having our pictures taken standing against a hanging sheet. No one had a clue why or what was going on, so most pics were unsmiling and a little defensive in posture. We didn't know what we were in for, and these obligatory photos felt like mug shots.

I'll begin with the ropes course. If you've ever enrolled in one of these heart-stoppers, you know what's coming. Let's call it a very effective method for facing fear head-on. This was no middle-school prefab plaster of Paris wall climb. This was the real deal — a series of terror and strength-challenging activities in rugged high mountain terrain, administered by a no-nonsense team of excuse-ignoring ropes experts. An eye-opening demonstration by the team leader gave us a preview of what we would experience the following day:

Our evening lecture ends earlier than usual, and the trainer invites a tall, flannel shirt, Timberland boots-clad Paul Bunyan type to the podium. This gentleman will be our team leader and point person for what he called "the ropes course." I'm unfamiliar with the term, so my ears perk up, thinking to myself with a smirk, "Ropes course? I don't recall seeing kink on the syllabus." Within moments, I realize no one will be tied up in a Fifty Shades of Grey-style romp. That's a different module. He's describing a series of not at all sexy strength and endurance challenges that could trigger some of our most terrifying fears. Mountaineer dude now has my undivided attention.

After defining some common ropes terms, Mr. Bunyan smiles, makes a few last comments, and says,

"Let's play a little game. I'm going to give you some simple instructions, and we'll see if you can follow them, ok?"

All nod, "Sure," "Yeah," "No problem."

"Ok, ready? Stand up."

All stand up.

"Sit down."

All sit down.

"Stand Up."

Again, all stand.

"Stand Up."

There's a shuffle, some stay standing, others sit down, then quickly and sheepishly stand back up.

"Those who sat down and got up, please remain standing. The rest of you may sit down."

In a flat, emotionless voice, he says, "If you do that tomorrow, you're going to die. Let's try again..."

And the process continues over and over with similar results. A few flunkies in the group continue daydreaming and mishear the instructions, again doing the opposite of what is requested. The response from the instructor becomes more emphatic and dire:

"YOU WILL DIE TOMORROW if you don't follow our directions to the letter. Do you hear me? You could be suspended by a rope a hundred feet over a jagged rock-filled cavern and if you decide you know better than your instructor, your chances of survival will be around 1%. Ok, people. We're going to go all night with this if necessary."

It wasn't necessary. The mention of being suspended a hundred feet over deadly terrain got people's attention, and now everyone was on the same page. Mr. Bunyan congratulated us on having realized our vulnerability and the fatal possibilities of doing anything other than what he instructed... and bid us goodnight.

8:30 AM — It's now the next morning, the run is done, my non-breakfast/snack is over, and the ropes team corrals us into a waiting school bus. We're off to the slopes! I tell myself, "This is going to be fun!" The mood on the bus is upbeat, people are laughing and chatting, and no one has a clue what lies ahead, save a faint memory of an annoying dude from the previous night shouting at us to pay attention or die. We're in the breathtaking Catskill Mountains, it's a warm sunny July morning, and the wildflowers are in full-bloom. What could go wrong?

After about a twenty-minute ride, our bus pulls into a dirt and gravel parking lot. The door opens with a hiss, all rise and one by one, we soon to be rope experts or cadavers step out into the sunshine. We gather around the side of the bus and listen to a short cautionary talk from our team leader about taking care while walking over the rough terrain and of course the ubiquitous reminder, "For your safety (and survival), pay attention and follow instructions."

Three instructors lead us up a path to a clearing that overlooks a gorgeous tree-filled valley. There's a tower and a long cable stretching at a shallow angle down several hundred meters to a clearing with a similar tower. To kick the day off with a fun adventure, our team is treating us to a high-speed zip line. Though we're not up in the clouds, the Catskills can reach as high as 4,200 feet, and we're at least 2,000 feet above sea level. No worries, this exhilarating ride requires only a moderate stomach for heights, and little strength.

One at a time, we strap into harnesses attached to an overhead pulley. There's a clear view of our destination at the end of the long cable, and all we have to do is push off and ride the line, zooming in the wind 'til we reach the bottom, safe and sound. No one has a problem with this fun ride, save a handful of folks who suffer from acrophobia. Once they realize they are in no danger and see people hooting and hollering as they fly over the valley at great speed and come to a gentle stop at the bottom, they bite the bullet and go for it.

But soon, the unspoken truth comes out — all of today's rope challenges are mandatory, no exceptions. As I mentioned at the beginning of this chapter, the purpose of an outing like this is to confront and overcome fear. Oh, how naïve are we out-of-shape city folks who imagined a ropes course to be like an afternoon at Six Flags Great Adventure! There is also no gradual buildup to the fear factor. Once our zip trip is complete, the crazy begins.

Our instructors lead us up a steep path to another clearing. There are two shoulder-height towers on either side of a gully, maybe fifty feet wide and about seventy-five feet deep. A line connects the two towers anchored to large trees. In a cheery voice, our team leader introduces this course as the Tyrolean Traverse. I survey the situation, and decide that though the gully is deep and scary, the traverse seems like no big deal — just another pseudo zip line, but straight across instead of downhill. No one is freaking out... yet.

A volunteer steps forward. It's the young man who finishes first on the 1K every morning. He's not cocky about it — he's actually supportive of us stamina-challenged runners that can barely finish and seems to be an all-around nice guy. He's also ripped and putting most of us thirty-somethings to shame with his six-pack abs, well-rounded pecs, and bulging biceps.

Since I've convinced myself, this is no biggie, I enjoy a brief sense of foolish relief. Our young Bruce Lee reaches up, clamping his carabiner onto a slider from which he will hang as he pulls himself along the line, hand over hand, traversing the gully. After checking the straps on his harness, he gives us a smile, a thumbs up, and pushes off. "This will be a snap," says the idiot narrator in my head. Kung Fu Freddy, makes it across in no time. Cheers erupt on the far side!

The rest of us clueless newbies think we're going to duplicate his athleticism. Sure, the first half of this run is effortless. You begin at the top side of a downward curving line, sliding along until you reach the midway point where your weight on the slider *pulls the line into a wide V shape. Then a little "uh oh" arises in your "beginning to see the problem" mind. Because a slider is not a pulley, there's friction. The friction is enhanced by your weight, and the difficulty of the next phase is enhanced by your shitty physical fitness. Beyond the midway point, you must pull yourself up the cable at a shallow angle that increases with every inch of progress. Easy peasy for the first half, crazy difficult for the second. The last five- or ten-feet dragging one's formidable weight up the line at a 45° angle can feel like an eternity for us out-of-shape slugs, with pain and hopelessness intensifying with every agonizing pull.*

It's easy to miss the difficulty watching the young Olympians zip their strong, lean bodies across with little effort. I got the "oh shit" wake-up call, watching several not-so-fit folks stall halfway across and begin to cry. Good luck with that ploy. They soon learn there is no quitting or towing you back, because there is no tow rope attached to you. You're on your own. Fear factor is now in full force. You can hang there whining on the line for the next week, but in the end, there are two choices: a) haul your butt across, no matter how painful, and finish the damn course or b) stay put and become the entrée for the soon to be circling buzzards.

To encourage us to rise out of hell, there is a team of cheerleaders on the finish side yelling encouragement, "Come on (your name), you've got this! You're a hero! You can do this!! Seven more feet! Six more feet! Five... four..." You get the picture.

Though I don't cry, nor do I quit, I stall and rest when the angle gets the best of me. I know there are jagged rocks below, but fortunately I'm facing up, so I can only see clouds, sky and the fucking line and slider. My arms are aching so badly they're almost non-functional. And yet... we all have to overcome our fear, pain, lack of strength, and dire hopelessness; we have to keep on hauling until we hoist our exhausted, limp bodies up that last 45° stretch.

As the finish line is almost within reach, and I decide death is not such a terrible alternative, I feel the first hands of a cheering fellow roper touch me, then everyone reaches out and pulls me up the last foot, cheering and shouting "Jimmy! Jimmy! You did it!! You are fearless!! Come get a hug!!" And the crowd surrounds and embraces me like I just survived a tragic shipwreck.

And that's the six-day course version of the Tyrolean Traverse. I'd like to say this chapter ends there, but nope. Next up...The Rappel! Again, this is not the YMCA, with a faux wall that you climb a ladder ten feet up one side and rappel down the other onto a mattress. This is a beautiful opportunity for cardiac arrest:

A team leader leads us up another long path to yet another clearing where we notice the trail ends a few feet ahead and the Catskill peaks rise in the distance...but...what...is...at...the...end...of...the... path? Soon enough we find out — nothing but air, a cliff and a hundred-foot shear drop. Maybe not a hundred feet, but if it was over twenty, the fear would be about the same. `Anchored into the rocks a few feet from the precipice, is a series of ropes. Another group of instructors are standing by, greeting us with warm smiles,

"Welcome folks! Ready to have some fun?"

"Dear God in heaven, what the fuck have you gotten yourself into?" says the now far humbler mental narrator, no longer cocky after the Tyrolean Traverse trauma. The "I'm the big man" fantasy has devolved into a medley of curse words in my head and under my breath.

The new humble and contrite me is standing somewhere around the middle of the line of nail biters, so I have ample opportunity to observe the terror. My classmates strap into their harnesses, one by one, each listening to the guide knowing their life depends on it. With futile protests facing the instructor and the El Capitan cliff behind them, they lean back over the edge and disappear into the void. Well, not exactly. There's a little step/hop thing you do as you ease yourself back and step horizontally down the cliff, inching the rope through your hands and belay mechanism to stop you from plummeting to your death. Several people just flat-out refuse.

"I can't do this. Sorry. No. Not doing it."

"I got it. You're scared. Now lean back..."

"NO!! You're not listening! I can't do this!

"I am listening. You're experiencing a little fear. Now lean back..."

"OMG, are you fucking crazy?? I AM NOT DOING THIS."

"I hear you, loud and clear. I've got you. You're safe. You can do this. Now lean back..."

The point is, we are being coached by a Borg. "Resistance is futile." The only way off that cliff is down the ropes. Period. The path back to the parking

lot is off-limits, and the bus left twenty minutes ago.
Fear is acknowledged but not accepted as an excuse
to turn back.

Every single one of us went over the side eventually, including a couple of old ladies. And… they weren't the ones screaming, "I can't do this!" They were brave and didn't say a word other than, "ok."

When it came to my turn, I had already seen the worst of the screamers and had a good idea what was coming. Though from where I was standing on the line, I could not see over the cliff and had only a vague idea what a hundred vertical feet looked like staring straight down. I imagined it might be like sticking your head out of a tenth-story window in an apartment building and looking down at the street below. Thankfully, I only had to do this once, because when you're repelling, you're looking up, not down, unless you're stupid enough to turn your head and upper body 180° and see how your life will end in a 2.5 second plummet, an agonizing scream, and a loud thud. So, if you choose wisely and remain looking up or at your feet against the cliff, you won't see how far down you have to go. You only see how far you've rappelled. To my amazement and delight, it was not a big deal and required little strength. You're holding onto ropes threaded through a belay or grab/release device that you manipulate to lower yourself down the cliff. It's comforting when you realize all you have to do is let up on the rope; the belay locks and you stop. That plus there are several trained assistants above that are holding on to the other end of a safety backup line attached to your waist. You can't fall. The worst is your feet slip and you end up dangling. Recovering is easy. You're flat against the cliff, so you push away with your feet, then on the return swing, step up to a horizontal position and release the belay a little at a time and resume inching your way down the cliff.

There was one hilarious moment when an older gentleman started shouting, "I can't do this anymore! I'm really scared, I'm out of breath, and my hands don't have much more strength. Please pull me back up!" Imagine his surprise when he heard a large group burst out laughing nearby. He was looking up, shouting to the team at the top and didn't realize he was eight feet from the bottom, just above their heads!

With the last rappeler touching down, the ropes course came to an end. The feeling of power and exhilaration among us was palpable. As cheerful, and clueless as we were on the ride to the circuit that morning, we were exuberant on the way home, trading stories and laughing at our missteps. We had faced life-threatening challenges, and not a single person was harmed, save a blister or two and an occasional rope burn on some hands. I salute the creators of this fantastic circuit for assisting my classmates and me to rise above lifelong fears and imagined inabilities. We did it!

Part 2: The Sex Module

We had no idea what was in store for us when we signed up for the six-day. The seminar descriptions were vague. Of course, practical stuff like food, lodging, hours, and ground rules were all covered, but what would be contained in the various modules was a closely guarded secret.

I'm sure if they had revealed that there would be an explicit module on sexual hangups, fears and anomalies and a pro level ropes course normally restricted to seasoned climbers, it would have thinned the herd down to a handful of diehard self-improvement junkies and a few idiots who weren't paying attention at the intro lecture. The EST team kept their cards close to their vests, and a decent sized group of us signed up, enthusiastic and naïve.

With that in mind, let's talk about the sex module. (Module is my word. Not sure if they even gave the sections names). When we learned of the day's subject, eyebrows went up, and smirks appeared on most faces, as well as jokes and chatter about what might be in store for us. Our trainer did his usual greeting, delivered some small talk about the previous day, answered a few questions and finally, introduced today's subject:

"Who among you has ever masturbated?"
Murmurs and mumbling, — "what did he just say?" "Wait, what??" "Get out of here…"
A few brave, liberated hands go up.

"Ok, let me phrase that a little differently — anybody who has never masturbated, please stand up."

WTF? Not a soul stands up. My jaw drops.

"Ok, anybody who has masturbated at one time or another in their life, please stand up."

All rise! I am thrilled beyond words. If I'm going to hell for "impure touch" as the Catholic priests liked to call it, I'm going to have a lot of company!

I've seen some clever ice breakers before, but this one takes the twenty-pound trophy. The mood in the room goes from cautious and nervous, to enthusiastic and ready to hit the ground running!

A large screen rolls down at the back of the stage. The trainer says, "What you're about to see are some very explicit sexual scenes. Some of them may offend you. Some of them might frighten you. Some of them might even get you aroused. All of them are required viewing — please honor your agreements and stay seated.

The lights dim and the movie begins. To create a gradual buildup, the first clip is a soft-core love scene with a hetero couple.

Let's pause this story for a moment. When I wrote the first draft of this chapter, it was a simple memory dump. I described the film in detail. Upon proofreading it, I realized it was way TMI and quite a sidetrack from my main purpose in this section — describing self-development through sexual healing. Instead, it was so hyper-pornographic, it would make a hooker blush. We had seen everything we could or could not imagine in sexual encounters between every combination of genders and numbers of humans (no animals, thankfully), and the result was quite surprising. There were no complaints and no expressions of disgust. We all cheered and applauded. I believe there was a standing ovation.

We didn't dwell on the film afterwards. Our trainer simply asked what everybody thought, almost as a rhetorical question. Nobody was offended, or if they were, they kept it to themselves.

"Great!" "Loved it." "Sweet!" Etc., etc.

It was a self-contained section, with a clear beginning and end. And what was there to say? Like the actors in the film, this episode came to a happy ending.

We're not done with sex quite yet, though. Question — what would a foray into your wildest sexual fears be without being required to detail your sex life and all your kinky fantasies and encounters in front of a group of complete strangers? Does that sound like a nightmare packed with humiliation and torture? Are you getting butterflies in your stomach and feeling a little nauseous at even the thought of that? I know I was when they announced we would be breaking into groups of eight, four men and four women, and doing just that.

For the first brave person to begin, I agree, it's difficult. You must decide if you're going all-in, complete honesty, open book, or... you're going to only frost the cake with vanilla icing and leave out the chocolate and raspberry inner layers. Our opener did no such thing. He was gay and gave us an insider's perspective on his and many of his friends' sex life, fantasies, toys, multiple partners in one evening, the works. What this did was set the bar quite low for the rest of us. Witnessing his bravery gave us the courage we needed to tell our unvarnished stories in all their embarrassing, gory details. By the third person, the camaraderie had grown to almost family. We listened to each person as they squirmed at first, then evolved into, "who gives a fuck? Here I am, emotionally naked and wide open." No one laughed, no one made unkind remarks, no one criticized, and we all thanked each other for showing courage and honesty in the face of tremendous fear. When these fantasies get dragged out of the dark cellar of our guilt-stricken minds and meet the clear light of day, the worst they appear is silly and harmless. Some are actually quite arousing. We were all thankful that no one expressed fantasies of rape, violence or deadly choking. This exercise was a life-changer.

Sexual hangups thrive in an atmosphere of guilt and shame. We are forced to endure conditioning from an early age by uptight parents, religious leaders, parochial schoolteachers, and sometimes, ignorant politicians. But mold dies in the sunshine. When you sit with a group of all ages, races, and sexual preferences, and you listen to admissions of sexual practices and fantasies that you can barely admit to yourself, leave alone to a group of strangers, there is a freeing of the psyche. It feels like the unlocking of handcuffs that you have worn since childhood. The experience is exhilarating. You may not leave the training fully liberated, but it is an enormous step in the right direction.

I'll finish this chapter on the Six-Day Course here. There were many other exercises, lectures and insights, but for this book, I think we've covered what's most interesting and pertinent. I enjoyed this course. The modules stirred up the gamut of feelings from terror to elation, from inspiration to boredom and everything in between.

One last fun thing. At the end of the course, we repeated the photo shoot. What a transformation! Now, everybody had positive body language and big smiles. Comparing the before and after pictures was quite illuminating. One was a representation of fear and mistrust, the other, joy and elation. What better way to send us home than a visual presentation of the change that happened over the previous six days?

The EST training has gone through quite a lot of evolution since its inception. After much criticism from the press and a smear campaign from L. Ron Hubbard (Founder of Scientology), the need for Werner Erhard to fashion a gentler approach gave birth to *The Forum*. Then in 1991, Erhard sold his existing intellectual property to his employees who adopted the name *Landmark Education*, and later in 2013 renamed the company *Landmark Worldwide*. As of this writing, Werner Erhard is eighty-eight years old, retired, and living in Pennsylvania.

Lifespring

To begin this chapter, I planned to quote from Wikipedia, as I had done in previous chapters, for a quick overview of the subject. Wikipedia is reliable for carefully-written and well-cited articles that are an enormous improvement over my memory. Not this time. With Lifespring, I'll only quote the first line of the Wiki page: "Lifespring was an American for-profit human potential organization founded in 1974 by John Hanley Sr., Robert White, Randy Revell, and Charlene Afremow."

After that, the article describes Lifespring as a cult, quoting various academic articles accusing the program of coercive techniques to prevent people from leaving and noting accusations of trainers hurling insults and humiliating some participants. True, but not in my case. I left the trainings mostly unscathed. The insults were directed towards people who were ignorantly stubborn and endlessly argumentative in accepting some simple basic concepts that were in my mind, well, basic, and quite true. If you came for coddling, you were in the wrong room.

The article also accuses Lifespring of relentless recruiting. True. Like EST, they used participants as an unpaid sales team. "Bring in your family." "Bring in your friends." And the best one, sell this program with "whatever it takes." No one liked the guilt-laden recruiting in Lifespring or EST, but those complaints did not tell the complete story.

For me, Lifespring was an effective eye-opener to some of my worst blind spots, i.e., my often-handicapped ability to see things as they are, and deal with them realistically. Call it a fertile, self-defensive imagination. Deflect and procrastinate. That was me.

I attended two trainings, The Lifespring Basic, and The Lifespring Advanced. I'll now take you to the training room so you may enjoy (or hate) the experience like a participant. First up — an eye-opening exercise from the Advanced:

About one hundred of us sit in a large circle, chairs near the wall. Our trainer, Lynn, a psychologist with an aggressive personality, asks couples to join her in the center of the room. Maggie and I oblige. She tells us to stand back-to-back. Then she says,

"Rate your relationship using your fingers, one to ten, with ten being the best. Hold your hands up, but don't share your rating with your partner."

She steps up to us. "You two are in big trouble. Turn around and show each other your hands."

Bloody hell, Maggie rated us a three, and I rated us a five.

In that simple test, Lynn gave us permission to declare in front of one hundred people that our marriage was on the rocks. We knew we had problems, but Lynn made it clear that if something didn't change soon, we were finished. Just taking part in that exercise and admitting our reality to the class gave both of us tremendous relief. We were no longer hiding our true feelings, and we had the support of a large group to work through our differences with absolute truth.

That was it. The class moved on to the next lesson without comment.

Basic Training, day two: an exercise/game. Think about the word, "try." Try to understand. Try to be on time. Try to use deodorant more often, etc. Lifespring taught that there is no trying. Our trainer insisted "try" is a meaningless word. Here's an example from the event:

John Webb, our trainer, speaks. "May I have a volunteer?" A man raises his hand. John calls him to the front and lays a pen on the floor.

"Try to pick up my pen."

The volunteer picks up the pen and hands it to John.

"I'm sorry, you misunderstood me. I said 'try' to pick up my pen," and places the pen back on the floor.

Again, the man picks it up.

"No, no, you're picking up the pen. Don't. I want you to 'try' to pick up the pen."

The volunteer is now looking confused.

Two more rounds elicit chuckles from the class.

The message is now clear: You're either doing something or you are not. There is no "trying."

Several people argued with John, but I had to agree. If someone tells you to try not to smile, you either smile or you don't. One might confuse trying with making an effort, but the end result is what counts. If you are making an effort to not smile and you succeed, then you didn't smile. If you failed, you smiled, thus you were doing one or the other regardless of the effort. Hence, there is no trying. You may "try" to lift a heavy barbell. No matter how much strain or ease, one of two things happens. You either lift the barbell or you don't. You may say you tried to lift it but couldn't. The fact is only one result occurred. You didn't lift it. If you still don't buy this conclusion, you may email your argument to Lifespring Customer Service at notworthit@whocares.com.

We also touched on the word "hope." Lifespring contends that hope is meaningless and has no power. They ask, "What events come into play when we hope?" "I hope I win the lottery." If I win, is hope responsible? "I hope you are not cheating on me," does little more than express one's feelings of possible betrayal, perhaps with an implied warning. It would be better (according to Lifespring) to just ask, "Are you cheating on me?" That question at least facilitates a course of action depending on a yes or no. I won't belabor this point. Let's get on with the deeper stuff. Here's another exercise:

Again, on the Advanced course, Lynn asks us all to choose a partner. The goal is to choose someone we don't like and discuss our issues with an open heart towards healing. My partner is David, a black man. I foolishly tell myself I have no prejudice, but damn if prejudice didn't seep into the interaction for both of us.

David: "You scare me a little."
Me: "I feel the same way."

We go into all our reasons, with complete honesty (a prerequisite), and it is remarkable how we end up. After some conversation we both realize our fears are ridiculous. I'm a harmless musician with marital problems. He's a Radio Shack salesman with a college degree and a steady girlfriend. He tells me he carries the legacy of past generations, enduring slavery, disrespect, segregation, etc. His parents drummed it into him to always be on the lookout for trouble where white folks were concerned. From my side, I was taught to hate, fear, and avoid black people. Their music was another story, though. In my youth, for example, I loved to listen to Little Richard and Ray Charles records. If my dad was within earshot, he would come into the room and shout, "Turn that screaming nigger music off!" That made David laugh, as he was also a fan of both artists, and could almost imagine his parents doing the same thing with a Perry Como or Lawrence Welk record. We acknowledged that with the best intentions for our safety and wellbeing, our parents had passed on their prejudices, infecting us, and dooming us to embody the same hate, disrespect and prejudice that they had inherited from their parents and grandparents.

One could pass this exercise off as superficial, impractical in real world interactions, and incapable of rooting out deep conditioning and long held prejudices. But I found it helped me to at least try (oops!) to take each person as they are without regard to my parents' fears. Of course, one simple exercise can't be expected to uproot years of parental programming, but we have to start somewhere. We can recognize the prejudice, and choose to not act on it.

By the way, my parents didn't limit their prejudice to black people. They were also not too keen when I dated Joy Wong, a Chinese Brazilian lady from São Paulo. I can't imagine how they would have reacted if I had introduced them to Ralphie Spiegel, a beautiful young black woman I dated in the late sixties. Ralphie had been adopted by Jewish parents, hence her unusual name, and Jews were also not on the most favored list around the Ryan household. That came into focus with my second wife. She was (is) Jewish. Oh, the temptation of the forbidden fruit! If my girlfriends weren't Irish Catholics, they were eyed with suspicion and our relationships were discouraged, to put it mildly.

While we're on the subject of prejudice, this next exercise set off a nuke in that deep, subconscious place where my nightmares are stored and triggered my *get out now* mechanism. I've mentioned that as a kid I was quite shy. I tended to not speak until spoken to. Here we go.

Trainer Lynn announces that it's time to put ourselves "out there." She tells us we will take a three-hour break, go out into the streets of New York City and choose a random person with whom we will convince to "break bread" with us and have a meaningful conversation. We should approach them unthreateningly, chat them up, as the Britts like to say, and invite them to join us for a meal or snack, but not a drink. We are also forbidden to reveal that we are on assignment from the training.

135

In very simple terms, I can't. I simply can't. I was horrible at picking up girls in my youth and was not prone to starting conversations with strangers at parties, but this? Approaching a random stranger in the "City of Paranoia" and thinking they wouldn't be spooked, or even call the police on me? My mind is racing, and I am not ready for this. But I'm all-in on this course, so cheating or lying, saying I completed the assignment when I didn't, is not an option for me. This is about integrity, and I'm not prepared to cross that line over a little (or a lot of) fear. But sweet Jesus, are you kidding me?

Suddenly, a solution comes to me like a heavenly blessing with a twofold benefit. As a snobby TM teacher, I tend to look down on spiritual practices and masters who I think are phony or less significant than our fab movement with its ten-thousand-year tradition. (Of course, that's an arrogant and ignorant point of view, but I had not come to that realization yet — not much better than my parents, I guess.) But then my target for the assignment materializes right there in my mind's eye — anyone from the Hare Krishna movement! What put that idea in my head? I have no idea, but I'm going for it.

I held some mighty judgmental views regarding these shave-headed, goofy dancing, finger cymbal clanging and chanting hippies. In the spirit of the life examination in which I'm currently enrolled, I believe this would be a great opportunity to examine my prejudice while checking off the assignment.

I mentioned a twofold benefit. Firstly, convenience. They have a center in Brooklyn a few subway stops away where I can walk in and just talk to whoever is on reception. Secondly, their center has a fabulous Indian restaurant, open to the public, where I can invite my person of interest to "break bread" with me and help me eliminate my bias and maybe gain some wisdom about their practice.

Out of the conference/ballroom, I march, a sly smile on my face, because in my head, I am about to crush the assignment without having to leave my comfort zone. I step up to the elevator... a few seconds... ding... the door opens, and I'm on my way. The elevator comes to a gentle stop as it reaches the ground floor. The door opens, and I stroll out of the building, walk two blocks, and descend the stairs down into the subway.

My ride is a little longer than I expected — about a half hour, but I'm in no hurry. After a few stops, I arrive at the Nevins St. station. Once I get upstairs, it's a short three-minute walk to 439 Henry Street. As I turn the corner, I see it — a beautiful six-story building in the middle of the block with a big black awning stretched out over the sidewalk from the front entrance, blazoning white letters that spell out "Hare Krishna Center."

I enter the building, and I'm immediately approached by what appears to be a young Indian woman in a sari. She greets me with a warm smile and in a soft, accented voice says, "May I help you?" Deep breaths. I'm a little nervous, but infinitely less so than if I was approaching a stranger in the waiting room at Grand Central Station. With a touch of shakiness in my voice, I tell her I'd like to talk to somebody about the Hare Krishna movement, that I had some possible misconceptions I wanted to clear up. She says, "I'd love to talk to you about this. Shall we sit down over there? I think we'd be more comfortable than standing here in the lobby."

That's my cue for benefit two. I say, "I've been told your restaurant is world renown, and I'm famished. Might we sit down there and have a bite and a chat?"

"Of course! I'll take you there."

We walk down a hall and then take a short flight of stairs down to what they call Govinda's Vegetarian Restaurant. It's not crowded, as it's the middle of the afternoon. We sit down at a random table. Paper menus are neatly assembled in a charming little handmade wooden rack, so I select one and scan what looks like a tantalizing selection of Indian dishes. A waiter in a saffron colored robe approaches, and with a faint Southern accent, asks if we're ready to order. I say sure, and choose a mixed vegetable curry and a mango lassi. My guide lady is not hungry, so she just orders a chai.

Now comes the hard part. I have to own my opinions and prejudices and tell my story in all its ugly glory.

"You seem kind and very approachable. I must confess, I felt a bit weird coming here. I expected you all to be chanting and trance-dancing in the lobby, but you seem very normal."

She is amused, but says nothing and lets me continue.

"I'm a TM teacher, you know, Transcendental Meditation from Maharishi Mahesh Yogi?"

She nods, but still does not comment.

"It's so easy to pass judgment when coming from ignorance, so I wanted to talk to someone from your group in hopes of becoming more familiar with your *practices and ridding myself of this burden of prejudice."*

I'm not sure why I'm using such formal words. Probably just insecurity, but then she finally speaks.

"Have you seen anything today that would make you feel uncomfortable?"

"No, quite the contrary."

"Wonderful. Please let me explain. We are a gentile congregation with no desire to make enemies. Our form of worship may seem strange to devotees of traditional Western religions, but we worship the same God as you do. May I assume you worship God?"

"Uh... yes, of course." I'm taken a little off guard by her question.

"Are you a Christian?"

"Yes... of sorts."

She smiles a knowing smile, realizing I may not be a practicing Christian, and continues.

"Well... our way of worship does not involve Jesus, though we respect all risen masters. We worship Krishna, whom I guess you might call a Hindu God. Are you familiar with the Hindu religion?"

"Yes."

"While you may sing hymns to Jesus, we sing, or shall I say, chant, to Lord Krishna. But we like to move as we do, so we dance and chime with finger cymbals. It is a wonderful experience. One loses one's self in the blissful reverie, and troubles fall away. In order to immerse one's self in this practice, however, there is an element that doesn't always resonate with the Western way of life — surrender. Many people find that difficult, but we have people

from all over the world who have taken that step and never regretted it. Our waiter, Shiva Ram, grew up on a farm in Kentucky."

I'm smiling, ear to ear, not because of her charming manner, but because I am realizing in real time how idiotic my prejudice is. This delightful woman is as normal as my sisters, and in another frame of reference, say on Fifth Avenue on a business day, if she was coming down the street, dancing, finger cymbals clanging, and chanting Hare Krishna, Hare Krishna with her group of devotees, I would think of her and her lot as complete weirdos. Not here, and not today. With her warmth, composure, and confidence, she is making me feel completely at ease, as if I was chatting with a close friend.

We must have sat there for over an hour, sharing our experiences of religion, friends, growing up, parents, etc., and I was genuinely disappointed that I had to rush back to the city to continue my Lifespring course.

"I'm sorry to end this wonderful conversation, but I have to be somewhere, and I must go."

Reaching across the table and taking her hands, I say, "I very much enjoyed our time together, and it has genuinely changed me. Thank you for that. I wanted to confront and get rid of my Hare Krishna prejudice, and you have helped me do just that.

With a smile, she says, "Lord Krishna has blessed us. Go in peace, my friend."

This little jaunt to Brooklyn started off as almost a cheat, like only reading the inside flap of a hardcover book in middle school to do a book report. My intention was to simply execute the task with as little stress as possible, putting myself "out there" but staying well within my comfort zone. I chose a place where I knew I would be welcome, and anyone would be happy to talk to me.

So no, I did not go up to a stranger on 51st Street and say "Yo — wanna snack down on a Dunkin Donut and chat?" What I thought was a mild cheat, ended up with my stumbling into a remarkable opportunity for psychological growth.

I sometimes entertain the delusion that I have control of my life. Do I hear laughter coming from the Universe? Yep. Damnit.

Ok, two last exercises from the Lifespring Advanced:

We've finished listening to a mundane lecture on a forgettable subject and are back in our chairs in the big, room-wide circle. We're still wearing our name tags.

Lynn says, "Take off your name tags, and place them in your pockets. Stand up. Form two semicircles. Those on the right, move clockwise. Those on the left, counter clockwise. You will stop momentarily to face each person in the opposite line and state one of two things, either their name, or the words 'I don't care enough about you to remember your name.'"

If this was the humiliation mentioned in the Wikipedia article, we now experienced it full-force. It's difficult enough to say those words to people you believe are insecure, sensitive, or easily hurt. But then when you rack up fifty to seventy-five people delivering the "I don't care enough about you" line to *you*, it is a humbling experience, especially for entertainers like me, whose career depends on large-scale recognition. This was a brilliant wake up call for narcissists who are so wrapped up in their own agendas, they don't even hear your name, leave alone remember it. I'm not a disinterested jerk, but I'm also not Mr. Memory. Remembering people's names was now a priority.

The final Lifespring exercise I will describe was similar to this, and as I recall, followed directly from the name game.

We're back in our seats feeling depressed after that name fiasco. Lynn, decides to brighten things up. In an uncharacteristically soft voice, she says,

"Close your eyes and let your imaginations run wild. You are on a luxurious cruise ship somewhere in the North Atlantic. The day has been relaxing, wonderful, and you are now enjoying a lavish evening meal with dear friends. The staff brings many courses of delicious food, cooked to perfection and served with the finest wines with each course. After long, wonderful moments of food and conversation, a server brings a tray of sumptuous desserts of every kind, something for everyone's taste.

"You remain at the table long after the meal is done, continuing pleasant conversations, but it's now time for bed. You hug your friends and make your way back to your cabin for a pleasant, deep night's sleep. Upon opening your cabin door, you

see an inviting, turned down bed, wrapped little mints on the pillows and a small, unopened bottle of after dinner wine. You get undressed, slip under the warm covers, pick up the crystal glass next to the bottle, getting ready to pour a delicious bedtime drink, and..."

BOOM!!!! Lynn hits the dais with her fists so hard everyone in the room jumps. Some women scream!

She speaks rapidly in an agitated voice, "Your ship has hit an iceberg! The lower decks are taking on water! Emergency warning sirens are blasting from the speakers at deafening volume in your room and the hallways! Everyone is panicking! The ship is sinking! Get to the lifeboats! Take nothing with you! You must move quickly or risk going down with the ship!

Lynn halts the story. "Everyone stand. We will again file into two concentric circles. As before, the circles will move in opposite directions. You will say to each person as you face them, either 'You go,' (on the lifeboat) or 'You don't go.' Simply put, you are saying you sentence them to death by drowning, because you don't care enough about them to save their life."

You think it was hard to tell someone they weren't important enough to remember their name? Imagine telling them they were so unimportant you sentence them to death. I believe the Wikipedia author felt this qualified as abuse.

"Lifeboat" proved to be a popularity contest. Most people did not make it onto a lifeboat, me included. The ones who made it were those who took part actively in the course, raising their hands often to ask intelligent questions. They were also the ones who were helpful and sincere in the small groups. With my marriage on the rocks and all the frustrations of my musical career, I confess I spent much of the course in my head, ignoring the best interests of others. I deserved my place in Davy Jones' Locker.

I loved this exercise. Again, such a brilliant wake-up call for how one behaves around others, while delivering timely karma for how one is perceived as a result of their behavior. Detractors might decide, "Who cares. I'll never see these people again." But then they forfeit an opportunity to see themselves in the mirror as others see them. In fact, most people rarely show that kind of honesty. It might be impossible to care about everyone we meet. But in normal conversation, is it so difficult to remember a person's name? Let's take it one step further. Beyond their name, if they're important enough to share a conversation, then why not listen to them with full attention? Hear them. Comment on what they say to you. Must we monopolize conversations? Is our opinion or agenda so important that we must interrupt, butting in with our view on the subject? Those kinds of interactions during the training influenced our classmates to either invite us into the safety of the imaginary lifeboats or leave us to shuffle the deck chairs as we meet our death by drowning. For me, it broke down to two questions. Is it all about me, or is it all about everyone in the conversation? I like the latter.

In my acknowledgments at the beginning of the book, I thanked John Hanley, one of the founders of Lifespring, for softening the blow I received from Werner Erhard's teachings. EST strengthened my ability to conduct and excel in business. But Lifespring helped me to favor the heart over the mind in personal and love relationships.

John Barton, Pseudotherapist

It's now 1981. I'm working as a staff songwriter at Atlantic Records' publishing company, Walden Music. My writing partner, Andy Goldmark and I are having some issues with our communication, and I'm having big issues with Maggie. Andy has a therapist named Sandra who he likes, and I ask him for her number. When I call, she expresses regrets she's maxed out on clients and can't take me on. She recommends a colleague, John Barton, and gives me his number. I call him — he is cordial, interested and available. We book a session.

I never worked one-on-one with a shrink before. My lightweight psych research revolved around reading Freud, Reich, Jung and others, but reading about their theories is a different matter than working with one of their students.

If you've never worked with a psychotherapist, it is much like how the books and satire present it. Maybe not lying on a couch staring at the ceiling and free-associating about your mother, but at the very least sitting across from the therapist and telling your story. For the most part I enjoyed and learned from the process, but one thing I found troubling with John was his sometimes-lame responses to my questions:

"Hey John, I had this weird dream last night. I dreamed that (blah, blah, blah) and I'm a little upset. It seemed so real, and it's still reverberating in my head. What do you think it means?

"What do *you* think it means?"

I hate this answer. There are many books published on the meaning of dreams. They are all a fraction of the cost of one session with a shrink. Why wouldn't he bring up some of the vast knowledge on the subject so we could engage in a productive conversation? A research-supported response might lead to my recalling even more of the dream, but no. "What do *you* think it means?"

I do my best to respond, but it doesn't help, because to make matters worse, he neither agrees nor disagrees with my answer. I could resolve the inquiry just as well with a journal entry. I'm pissed, and I believe a little red flag just popped up.

On the positive side, John mostly understands my issues and offers insightful guidance (as long as we aren't talking about dreams). He helps me see through some of my delusions, assists me in eliminating some self-destructive patterns, and gives me sound advice about the consequences of coddling my foibles and not confronting them. What foibles, you ask? Here's one:

Maggie and I have sexual problems. On the enthusiasm scale, I'm all in. She's all out. What I'm now learning is that aversion to sex often has its roots in anger. I know only too well that Maggie feels angry about a lot of things in her life, none the least me. But I never made the connection that sexual desire for someone was inversely proportional to one's anger towards them. What have I done to make her so angry? One obvious answer is I have a mistress — my work. Because I'm a songwriter and an active musician, my day job often spreads into the night, and Maggie spends a lot of time alone while I work... and work... and work. I want to be the best. I'm a perfectionist, and I craft my musical creations with an unhealthy dose of oversized ambition, hoping each one will break me into higher and higher echelons of "the biz," i.e. advertising, hit records or building the best high-end project studio in NYC.

John warns me that my workaholism will doom my marriage if I keep it up, but I can't seem to tear myself away. My career is my life, and competing in NYC can be like swimming up a waterfall. It is exhausting. But if salmon can do it, I can do it. Like an idiot, I expect Maggie to understand this and support me. On the surface she does, but underneath, in her subconscious, a storm is brewing, time is running out for us, and sex is off the table.

(A few months later) Maggie's anger and her reluctance to be intimate with me have now so alienated me I'm halfway out the door. But I'm brainwashed by the Catholic belief that marriage is forever, complicated by the fact that there are no divorces in my family. Nonetheless, my commitment is crumbling. John coaches me through this period, but an unfortunate event prevents us from completing our work.

His colleague, (Andy's therapist) Sandra, is sponsoring a weekend retreat at her home in an upscale New Jersey neighborhood on the Hudson River. John and his clients have been invited to join Sandra and her clients. We're a medium sized group of around thirty people. About two hours into the retreat, I notice something odd — Sandra is doing all the talking. John is neither contributing, nor has Sandra invited him to do so. She hasn't even introduced him. He just stands silently in the corner of the room, observing, but not commenting on anything we share. His behavior is strange, and he looks worried. Though this is not the John I know, I'm too caught up in my own mental machinations to bother asking him what's going on. Sandra is doing such a great job, it almost doesn't matter... almost.

Sandra takes us through a number of exercises, enquiries, duets and psychological prods to open up the areas of pain we've been concealing for years. Her methods are very effective. Almost everyone responds in positive ways, but of course there are the holdouts — the ones who are just too shut down to respond to this kind of interaction. I'm grateful that I am not one of them, and for me the weekend goes very well. I work out my communication problems with Andy, as well as several other issues that were troubling me, the details of which are unimportant.

Yes, I'm being a little vague, because this retreat, its methods, and its results are not the primary focus of this story. Something that came out of the weekend is. Keep reading...

We all leave Sunday late afternoon with smiles on our faces, getting into our cars and heading home with newfound enthusiasm for what lies ahead in our personal and business lives. I'm ok, but I'm concerned about John. He left before the retreat's ending, and as far as I could tell, did not say goodbye to anyone. I'm feeling uncomfortable, and I want to know what's going on.

In the following days, I make several attempts to contact him with no success. I get his answering service and leave messages, but he doesn't return my calls. Something is wrong. Trying to get information from Sandra proves fruitless, as she's also ghosting me.

Two weeks go by, and my patience hits its limit. I call Andy, who is still seeing Sandra, and vent my frustration. He agrees to ask Sandra why I'm getting the silent treatment, and the truth comes out.

Most psychologists and psychotherapists, paper their walls with diplomas and documents certifying their right to practice analysis and guidance. John's walls were bare. His diplomas were all in his mind. When I signed on with him, I never asked if he earned a master's or doctorate or where he got whatever degree he held. He seemed knowledgeable and had a good sofa-side manner, so I entered this relationship like a clueless dumbass. I did no research on him, no checkups with the New York State Education Department Office of the Professions, no recommendations from his current or former clients, nothing. But he seemed like a nice guy. What could go wrong?

Sandra was avoiding me because she was embarrassed. She felt she had failed in her fiduciary duty to screen John before recommending him to anyone. John's silence at the retreat and afterwards resulted from her having a suspicious interaction with him involving questions to which he should have had answers but did not. As a result, she went to the NYC board to check his credentials. The result? He had none. John Barton earned a bachelor's degree in liberal arts from some little-known college and did a stint in the army. But my would-be shrink had no psychotherapy credentials whatsoever. I had been sharing sensitive personal information and pouring my heart out to a fraud posing as a Freud.

This mind-boggling discovery shakes me to the core. Who is this guy? Is my private information being leaked to some dark underworld crime organization to which he is a member? Would secrets I shared with him come back to bite me in the ass? Embarrassment? Blackmail? No degree, no client/therapist bond of confidentiality? My imagination and paranoia are pinning the meter. Maggie, normally tough and world-wise, is losing it. Our problems are hard enough without this bombshell from the gods of bad news. I can't just write his deceit off and walk away — I have to confront him.

Doing my best to stay calm, I rationalize that in many ways, he did help me. Maggie agrees. Regardless of his experience and poor judgment, his intuition was solid, as was his advice. I try to visualize him, not as a lying bastard, not as a dangerous criminal, but as a bit of a loser, just trying to get by the best he can. It works. That evaluation turns out to be the truth. Once he finds out I'm aware of his scam, he agrees to see me.

I grab a taxi to his Park Avenue office and ring the bell. As he opens the door, I see a new John Barton. In the past, he had always carried himself with confidence and dignity. Now he just looks sad and dejected. He leads me into his office with slumped shoulders and we sit down facing each other. Apologetic, open and honest, he admits his deceit. Though he makes excuses for his bad choices, it doesn't matter. We are done. I thank him for his service, tell him I'm not angry, just disappointed, and we both agree our relationship has come to an end.

I learned something valuable from my time with this man. People can be helpful to us during life's challenges without having received an advanced degree in psychology. They may not have all the answers, but neither do many professionals. In the end, it's up to us. Our therapists, priests, gurus, parents, siblings, relatives, lovers and friends can help and sometimes point the way, but it's our job to decide what's useful advice and what is not. We alone must make the tough decision to face or ignore what lies in the dark recesses of our psyches. If we give in to fear and resist parting those curtains, we sleepwalk through our lives. We remain stuck in our self-destructive habits until we can muster the courage to take the next step toward recovery, however small or large that step may be. For me, facing my problems and experiencing the associated pain was far easier than spending an entire lifetime in self-destructive cluelessness. It was like driving a car with a muddy windshield and no wipers. I like the old adage, "just rip off the bandage;" you may feel a sharp pain at first, but then… relief.

John Gray/Barbara DeAngeles

Making Love Work Workshop

This course was a lot of fun. Its purpose was to create a forum for couples to upgrade their relationships and learn valuable communication skills, bringing them closer to the love they shared when they first met. It also provided tools to eliminate clashes that undermine love and cause couples to drift apart. A married couple, Dr. John Gray, author of *Men Are from Mars, Women Are from Venus*, and Dr. Barbara DeAngelis, author of *Secrets About Life Every Woman Should Know*, created and facilitated this powerful workshop.

Despite having warm fuzzy feelings about the course, I recall almost no details, save a kind of frightening interaction that bore little relation to the subject of love and relationships. That plus one other high-level transgression that I will describe in a moment.

Here's what happened. A very rich and prominent socialite/heiress named Monica attended the course. I knew her from the TM circuit and liked her very much. Monica was a tall, attractive blonde, soft-spoken, dignified, and a portrait painter by trade. Unlike most people, she made a habit of maintaining eye contact throughout conversations. Talking with her was a pleasure. She would always give me the impression that I was the most interesting person in the room when we spoke. Monica came here with her fiancé, Leonard, hoping to resolve their relationship issues. Leonard, an athletic looking six-footer, well dressed and handsome with an easygoing, but slick manner, was an heir to an even larger fortune. He acknowledged their problems, but did not share her interest in resolving them in a group environment. Unsure what to expect from Monica's friends and this unfamiliar environment, he brought his longtime friend, Steve, to have his back if the psychological prying got out of hand. Steve was not slick. He had a rougher look, someone you would not expect to be hanging out, leave alone best friends with a mega-wealthy heir. He seemed out of place and uncomfortable in the group, keeping a low profile in the back row. Neither Leonard nor Steve knew what having one's back might entail, but Steve agreed to just show up and give Leonard moral support. Though Monica and Leonard had been a couple for many months and were now engaged, she met this alleged *lifelong* friend, Steve, for the first time this evening.

About a half hour into the course, during the go around, Monica and Leonard stood up and described their concerns and communication problems with each other. While Monica's description seemed typical of many relationships, Leonard's brought tears to our eyes. His communication problems, he told us, began during his tour of duty in the Vietnam war. He had seen buddies killed, arms and legs shot off, gangrene and so many other horrors. Tears ran down his face as he related details of the hideous war. We all gave Leonard our undivided attention.

Keep in mind, these workshops are designed to be safe spaces and thrive on truth and sharing deep insecurities. Upon completing his war story, Leonard shared that his social status, success and inheritance made little difference to him. Defending our country meant more to him than anything, and giving his life would be an honor if that's how things shook out.

We all applauded, giving him hugs and much admiration. Leonard's war story created an atmosphere of courage and honesty which should have helped others to come forward and share how their life experiences impinged on their relationships. Honesty and courage — that's what Leonard embodied. He wore it like a Purple Heart.

A few more brave course participants shared their feelings and worries about their relationships, but while they were talking, I noticed something odd was going on with his friend Steve. He looked concerned and agitated. Steve had been quiet and subdued until this point, but that was about to change. He raised his hand. John invited him to introduce himself and address the group. He stood up, looked at Leonard, then at Monica, shook his head and spoke:

"I'm Steve, Lenny's friend. Lenny, I'm sorry, man. These are good people. Monica is a dream lady and deserves your respect, and I just can't let your story stand. When I'm done, you might not want to be friends anymore, but your bullshit has crossed a line. First, we grew up in Brooklyn. You are not an heir to any fortune. Your name sounds famous, but you aren't. Your dad is a car salesman, and your mom is a school teacher. When you told me about the crap you fed Monica, I decided to let that little crock fall apart on its own over time, friends and all. But that speech you just gave pissed me off, big-time. You're full of shit, Lenny, and I've got to call you on it. You

never set foot in Viet Nam. For that matter, you were never in the service. You lying son-of-a bitch — you just jerked all these people around, and I can't figure out why, but I also can't let your bullshit stand, friends or no friends. What the fuck, man??"

"Monica, I'm sorry. We don't know each other, but you seem like a nice lady. You don't deserve to be lied to like this. (He looks around the room) Neither do you guys. Lenny — you asked me to have your back, but not like this, bro. I can't. Let's go man. We got no business being here."

The room fell silent, all eyes on the two men — one angry, yet confident about his disclosure, the other mortified that he had been busted. Leonard stood up, grabbed his jacket off the back of his chair, and without as much as a glance at Monica, made his way to the door and let himself out. Steve followed, stopping at the door and turning around. With a somber face, he looked at us, then at John and Barbara, nodded and slipped away into the night, leaving us with our heads ready to explode.

The two Brooklyn men were gone, but the unmasking of Leonard, a real-life predator, raised this lovemaking course to a new level of crazy. Monica had shock written all over her face. She was neither stupid nor gullible, but Leonard had gotten one whopper over on her. Until this astonishing revelation, blind love and passion almost had her marrying a complete fraud, putting her and her family's fortune within reach of a confidence trickster, and possibly endangering her life. She didn't know whether to cry or scream. In seconds, her poise and composure crashed, and she crumbled into a pile of rage, disbelief, horror and grief. We all got up and surrounded her, holding her hands while she cried her eyes out.

John and Barbara showed amazing skill, consoling her and bringing her around to the realization that what happened proved far more fortunate than if she had not attended the course and proceeded with the marriage. It's hard to find the good side of being duped, but if there was one, John & Barbara had it ready to go, and within a short time, things came back to normal, and we resumed the curriculum. No one was in a hurry, though. This was epic drama, and we were leaning in for every second of it.

Now the other event — a quirky exercise I remember with equal shock.

We're in a large room, maybe fifty of us. Our chairs are lined up in rows like a classroom, with John and Barbara up front. Barbara asks us to grab our chairs and spread out to allow as much space as possible between ourselves and other participants. Everyone picks up their chairs and heads for the walls. Barbara then tells us John will be turning off the lights. In the darkened room, we are to quietly express our feelings about our partner, what we love about our relationship, and what we would like to improve. The idea of separation and darkness is to ensure almost complete privacy. Everybody will be talking at the same time, so it will be difficult to comprehend what anyone else is saying. That, plus we're supposed to be talking, not listening. Maggie and I are not doing great at this point in our marriage, so I begin my monolog with a litany of our relationship foibles that could use improvement. She moves to the farthest place in the room, so neither of us knows what the other is saying. The room sounds like a busy theater before a performance. One can hear a mash-up of conversations, but nothing distinct because everyone is talking simultaneously in hushed voices. Occasionally, a familiar word like "love," "darling," or "bastard" will pop out, but mostly it's a cluster of unintelligible hash.

At first, many of us are a little shy and at a loss for words, but Barbara and John are wandering around the room whispering to us,

"Go deeper!"

"Tell them how you feel. Don't hold back!"

"There's more."

"This is the time to get it all out!"

"This is a safe space!"

"No one is listening to you; you can be honest."

Their encouragement works well. I start chattering on and on like I'm leaving a long voicemail. After about ten minutes, the lights come on. I look around and notice there is a distinct change in the room. Everyone's formerly hard New York street faces now reveal a softened glow, like the Six-Day EST course, quite an improvement over the skepticism and fear masks we wore on the way in. Complete honesty in a safe environment will do that, but there was more to it. It isn't like telling the truth in a shrink's office. This was fifty people all telling the truth at once. It's a real crowd changer, and this group now has morphed into a cohesive almost family. I say almost because I mean a warm, functional family, not the kind that curses their ancestors and throws drumsticks and stuffing at each other at Thanksgiving dinner.

Unfortunately, one little incident tainted this exercise. Many years after the course, my friend Philip and I were sharing our feelings about it all. I was praising it to the sky, but he countered my feelings with a little bomb. During the "blackout, tell-all" exercise, Barbara DeAngelis spent a good amount of time coaching him to spill his guts about everything that was going on in his heart. Phil quietly voiced feelings that were quite private and personal, meant for his own therapy and healing, things he would never have told his wife, Susan. Barbara later took Susan aside and told her almost everything that Philip had said in that alleged "safe space." If I had known that, I would have busted her in front of the entire group and walked out on the spot. Sadly, her indiscretion went unchallenged. Susan didn't tell Philip until weeks after the course, so the opportunity to confront Dr. DeAngelis was long gone.

I'm chuckling to myself as I write this, imagining Susan using what she learned in this indiscretion as evidence against Phil in their divorce proceeding. And yes, their marriage did not survive. Both have moved on and are now in more life affirming relationships.

As for Maggie and me, we enjoyed the course and felt encouraged by what we had learned. For a few months, we practiced John & Barbara's techniques to resolve conflicts and diffuse anger, but like the EST and Lifespring trainings, the effects of the course eventually wore off, and we settled back into our rut. As you may have guessed, our marriage did not survive. It didn't die a tragic death, though; it just faded out, and we walked away from it,

159

enthusiastic about our separate lives and ready to start over.

I won't spend any more time on this course as you can find a wealth of info on it and the subject of relationships from John Gray's and Barbara De Angelis' websites, as well as John's Audible version of the entire course with all its advice and techniques.

An odd twist to this story would fall into the category of "Do as I say, not as I do." John and Barbara didn't last as a couple, either. They taught hundreds of people how to make love work, but couldn't make it work for themselves. Neither could we. The Grays' marriage ended in 1984, Phil and Susan's in 1985, and my marriage to Maggie ended in 1986. But this is not as tragic as it sounds. In the end, we all found new partners who were a better fit, and though the path may have been painful, the final result feels like a perfect conclusion to this wild and crazy workshop.

Krishnamurti on Beliefs

In my pursuit of any and all forms of alternative spiritual thinking, I spent a short period in the early 70s reading the works of the Indian philosopher, lecturer, and spiritual teacher, J. Krishnamurti. From Wikipedia:

Jiddu Krishnamurti was an Indian philosopher, speaker, writer, and spiritual figure. Adopted by members of the Theosophical tradition as a child, he was raised to fill the advanced role of World Teacher, but in adulthood he rejected this mantle and distanced himself from the related religious movement. He spent the rest of his life speaking to groups and individuals around the world; many of these talks have been published. His books have sold over four million copies and are available worldwide in twenty-two languages.

Krishnamurti had a unique and peculiar mission. He encouraged his students to consider a quantum shift in the way they held their views. He dared them to discard their beliefs, to break free from conditioning. For most people, beliefs define their lives; they are central to their very existence and who they are. Some say without their beliefs, they would be nothing. For those of this persuasion, letting beliefs go is a non-starter. In my frame of mind, though, I was open to testing the premise. As I've mentioned many times in this book, the dogma to which I was subjected in my childhood felt like poison sandwiches. I was forced to eat them over and over. So, in my often, a little too enthusiastic and maybe not so sensitive way, I proposed the following to anyone who would listen:

A belief is something one accepts as true or real; a firmly held opinion or conviction, this according to The New Oxford American Dictionary. And I added to that definition, "without proof." If there is proof/evidence, the belief is verified and is recognized as a fact or truth.

The response was usually something like, "Yeah, so what? I know that (their belief here) is true. I just know it. I don't need proof. I have faith!"

My challengers would often argue about beliefs as if they were truths, even when facts contradict their convictions. You only need to look at modern politics to verify that scenario.

Example — a run in I had with a man in an Irish pub when I lived in London; I don't know how I let myself get dragged into an argument about religion, but I did:

"Oh, you can be bloody well certain there's a hell, and you, Jim, are well on your way with that rubbish you're spewing!"

"Really? Tell me, where is hell located?"

Silence... (His eyes squint slightly). "What kind of daft question is that?"

I continue with mild condescension: "Did archeologists or astrophysicists recently locate it?"

Crickets... (A frown now forming).

"And where did you learn about hell?"

He responds with righteous indignation: "In church and from the Bible, you heathen sod. Where do you think?"

Now he's pissed me off and I'm going for it.

"Is hell mentioned in the Old Testament?" (His fists now slightly clenched. His frown now a glare. I'm thinking wisdom might dictate not pushing this too much further... but screw it. I do anyway)

"Who wrote the Bible, and which of the approximately nine-hundred English translations is correct?"

Before he could answer, a mutual friend steps up to join us, and with a grin, says, "What are you two mindless twats prattling on about?" The interruption saves the day and perhaps my teeth! We leave it there, order another round, and change the subject.

Of course, there are few who can answer that last question outside of theological academia, and even with that lot, it would likely lead to endless arguments. It's probably best not to throw it in the face of someone who's on their third pint at the pub. Arguments about religion and politics are pointless, and can be dangerous in pubs, but I guess I'm a slow learner.

I engaged in verbal bouts with my sister right up to her death in 2024. We could never agree, and sadly, it came between us. It never should have... but it did. I agree with J Krishnamurti — beliefs can tear families, marriages, friendships and business relationships apart. They can also prevent otherwise desirable relationships from forming. So why do we cling to them? Do we actually need them? Is it hope, a yearning for something to define our lives? A need to belong to or be associated with some idea or organization we think is worthwhile? Probably all the above. I insisted as a kid that the Beatles were the greatest band that ever hit an E chord. My sister wouldn't listen to them.

In this brief study, I explore the idea that the negative effects might make beliefs more trouble than they're worth. I had no intention of abandoning all my beliefs, though. My elimination targets were passionate political, historical, and religious beliefs. Let me present a few questions I considered.

1. Can beliefs destroy relationships?

"I believe you cheated on me. We're finished. I'm breaking up with you."

"I did not. Who told you that?"

"That girl over there."

"Really? You mean the one that's had the hots for you for months?"

"Uh… I don't know about that, but yeah."

"And the evidence?"

"Well, Don's car was in your driveway yesterday…"

"Yes, he drove Bob over to see my sister."

"Yeah but… but…he was in your house…

"Yes, we talked. So what? My parents were home. WTF do you think happened??

Crickets.

This scenario happened to me in high school, and in acting on my belief, I dumped a wonderful girlfriend and did not take up with the accuser, who was a bitch and a witch, despite her hots for me. I had no evidence, and my girlfriend had plausible denial. My friend, with whom she allegedly cheated, denied the accusation and never pursued her. As for me, I foolishly jettisoned a great relationship based on my dumbass belief.

How many relationships have been destroyed by political beliefs? How many friendships end the second the news breaks that one is a member of the *other* political party? How many friendships never begin when different races, religions, or political beliefs are revealed?

What if we held our beliefs like unproven theories, with an open mind that we could be wrong? How would that affect our egos? Why are we so adamant about being right? What do these beliefs cost us in our pursuit of happiness? Who do you enjoy being with more, the person who is argumentative and always right, or the person who considers what you are saying and respectfully lets you have your opinion?

2. Can beliefs be deadly? Can they be profitable?

"I believe China is our enemy!"

"Why?"

"I see it all the time on the news."

"Is that an iPhone in your hand?"

"Yeah, why?"

"You realize that iPhones are assembled in China, don't you?"

"Hmmm. I did not know that."

"Have you ever heard Tim Cook, the CEO of Apple, declare China our enemy?"

"Well… actually… no."

"Do you know any Chinese people?"

"Sure. I've got a couple of Chinese friends. I used to date a Chinese girl."

"Were any of those Chinese people your enemy?"

"Of course not."

"Has China declared war on us?"

"Not that I'm aware of."

"Is it possible that your fear of China is based on political propaganda?"

"Maybe."

The protagonist continues: "Keep an open mind. China, despite the ongoing political animosity, is one of our greatest trading partners and the source of a vast amount of our manufacturing and technology. Perhaps we can be observant and open to threatening changes without spreading paranoia and hostility. Sure, they send an occasional spy balloon across the Midwest. And we jam it, then shoot it down when it's over water where the falling debris won't land on our heads. So, no biggie. Keep those iPhones coming."

Belief in political views is not *always* evil or dangerous. One can simply vote based on one's preference, at least in democratic nations. It's when one makes life decisions and forms hardcore opinions based on propaganda that the trouble begins. When money and power are involved, as they usually are in politics, the flames of fear, furor and passion grow geometrically, fanned by the opportunist media. From the lips of Dick Salant, former president of CBS News, "Good news doesn't sell." Note the word, "sell."

The belief that communism or Nazism is evil and capitalism is good or vice versa is an excellent war-starter. It worked well in the twentieth century and was effective in killing between fifty and eighty-five million people — not so much the politicians who started the wars (Hitler killed himself). Gone are the days of kings fighting on the front lines.

Imagine a world where people simply preferred their political party or system rather than believed it was supported by God, and anything else was inherently evil. With the warped egos corrupting and manipulating governments and political conversations, is that even possible? Or... is all that alleged corruption just my belief? It certainly gets my hackles up when I read about it. Click, ka-ching, click, ka-ching, click, ka-ching. The media earn ad money every time we click, so they keep those biased horror stories coming in... and we doom-scroll.

3. Can fervent beliefs lead to torment and anxiety?

Here are a few that fit into the mental torment category:
- Have I been good enough to go to heaven?
- Was that a mortal sin?
- I'm sure she cheated.
- If you believe (your belief here), you are not my friend.
- EMF is rotting my brain.
- Smart electric meters cause cancer.
- Ear buds cause cancer.
- Wind turbines cause cancer.

• Masturbation and blindness go hand in hand (pun intended).

• Aliens are walking among us and will soon take over.

At one time, we burned witches at the stake, engaged in the Spanish Inquisition, and marched in the Crusades. We committed senseless murders based on beliefs, many of which some still hold today. How about suicide bombers and terrorists declaring jihad based on their religious beliefs?

Some of the above will make you laugh or might even trigger you, but I had to ask myself, what do I believe that is causing me or others anxiety? Can I take that belief and explore the possibility that it may not be true? Could I consider converting it to some lesser probability and move it out of the frightening fact column? Any chance I could take a giant leap of faith and try not giving a shit about some things I previously believed? And as for you, dear reader, could you at least entertain the possibility that many of your beliefs have no supporting evidence? Would you consider doing exhaustive research to test them and abandon them if they prove to be false?

Imagine how liberating it could be to loosen that strangle-hold on our beliefs. Imagine being able to accept the possibility of being wrong, without self-judgment, just a simple, "oh well," and move on. That, I can assure you, would be an epic life-changer, an open-hearted walk in the fresh air of not having to engage in endless arguments, often in our own heads.

4. Could abandoning many of our beliefs lead to peace and freedom?

Returning to the Krishnamurti line of thinking and giving credit where credit is due, this is what I find compelling. How about living with an open mind, an open heart, no hard fixed position on the nonsense dividing us and simply listening to those who are troubled, who just need to be heard? For me, that is freedom, because with open hearts, we are not part of the conflict. Our opinions are not frozen. We are constantly open to updates and fresh possibilities. We are alive and vital in the present moment, the only moment that exists. It is difficult, if not impossible, to have no opinions, but it is possible to hold them loosely. I'm not talking about life-threatening situations. I'm talking about the day-to-day arguments we see, hear, and engage in on social media, in coffee shops, and at corporate water coolers. Can you imagine how that might improve your perception of each encounter when not being viewed through the equivalent of Vaseline-smeared glasses? Do you really want to be part of the never-ending struggle, defending pure fantasy?

In closing, consider this — with an open heart and mind, few hard fixed beliefs, just hypotheses, you sacrifice nothing. If your fantasy or hypothesis proves real, you're good to go. If it proves false, you're good to go. On the other hand, if you are a do-or-die believer, and life proves you wrong, you lose. You experience humiliation and defeat.

If this chapter tickled your curiosity, you can find many of Krishnamurti's books on Amazon, Barnes & Noble and anywhere fine books are sold. And I don't get a commission for including that last sentence!

Dr. Yvette Obadia
Psychotherapy on Steroids

My second wife and I had control issues. After endless King of the Hill arguments about who would drive, where we'd go, what restaurant, what TV show, what movie, what vacation, who got to hold the remote, we agreed to exchange days on which only one of us made the rules. It worked for a while, but sooner or later, the arguments resumed. We needed help, and on the advice of a friend, we sought counseling from a NYC psychiatrist, Dr. Yvette Obadia. It went very well at first, and then it took a wildly unexpected turn. Here's the story:

Dr. Obadia is not an ordinary psychiatrist. Her ways can be mysterious and opaque, and though I don't always agree with her, I go along with what she advises until I can no longer do so.

First the odd stuff. In my private sessions with her, sometimes, after a discussion of a painful memory, she abruptly ends our conversation by raising her index finger to silence me. Then she waves her hands in the air, says a few prayer-sounding words in a language I do not understand, and concludes,

"It is done."

"What is done?"

"It is done!"

Without an explanation, we move on. For me, sometimes it's done; sometimes it's not. But Dr.

Obadia comes highly recommended, so at least for now, I respect her technique, and we continue with a new subject.

On the less opaque side, she has a brilliant trick to settle tough issues between couples. It bears some similarities to Eckhart Tolle's pain body theory (detailed in A New Earth) but has some distinct differences. When an issue arises, one of us may declare, "I need fifteen minutes." That means the other has to sit silently for however long it takes the accuser to air their grievance, usually under fifteen minutes. Then, the other must not respond for twenty-four hours. After a day, the resentment almost always cools down, and it's easier to have a more reasonable conversation about the complaint. That part works well.

What doesn't work so well is the seething that takes place in the immediate aftermath of the complaint. Because the accused cannot speak or defend, they often feel resentful for at least the following hour. Though it is an argument-free way to air grievances, "I need fifteen minutes," is a mood killer, not to be used in the bedroom or during a nice dinner. Its intended purpose is to avoid arguments, and it works well for that, but the moment one invokes it, the other inevitably goes into a funk as they listen to the rebuke, psychologically muzzled.

Dr. Obadia insists on our meeting with her separately for the first month or two, eventually seeing us together. I'm fine with that. When we're alone, I can voice my complaints without resistance and receive some valuable insight. Or in other words, I can rage-dump with impunity. Those sessions go well.

The trouble begins when we start seeing her together. She seems overly sympathetic towards my wife. It's a disturbing turnabout from our private sessions.

And now, the troubling twist. Sex had become a problem (again). I'm interested in enjoying it often; my wife, not so much. A sexless marriage is a non-starter for me, so I bring the subject up, eager for a solution or at least some tips to start us on a way to recovery. Dr. Obadia listens but holds back her opinion for a moment. Then, looking back and forth between us, she drops the bomb.

"You have no 'right' to sex, regardless of marriage vows. Sex is never a guarantee, and under the circumstances, you must not ask for it."

What circumstances is she referring to? This vexing response is like a "fifteen minutes" from hell, and my pain body is now wide awake, claws out, and ready to fight. It never gets the chance, because she drops this maddening declaration at the end of our session. I feel hurt, deflated, and kicked to the curb, but my determination to resolve our issues prevails.

Though I still respect her, my opinion is Dr. Obadia crossed a line in taking such a heavy-handed, one-sided position. Marriage might not guarantee the right to physical intimacy, but we can't even talk about sex? Not a word? What have I done to deserve this ultimatum? What issue between us is so insufferable that Dr. Obadia felt the need to read me my Mirandas? i.e., you have the right to remain silent!

No one is talking.

With this unacceptable (for me) patient/doctor dilemma and my forking out today's equivalent of

172

about $400/hr., I tell my wife I no longer have faith in Dr. Obadia's judgment. Both she and Dr. Obadia express disappointment, but all agree to discontinue our therapy sessions.

For a while, we cruise along, pretty much the same as we always have, Halloween with the kids, Thanksgiving with her family, Christmas, etc., and I believe we're making some progress. But then on New Year's Eve, after a muted celebration, my wife declares,

"I'm not happy. I don't know if our marriage is going to survive, and from now on, sex is out of the question."

Yes, we have communication and control problems, but I didn't think they were deal breakers. I still love her, so I continue my efforts to repair the relationship, but I'm flying blind. She's not telling me what is wrong. All she offers is, "We're just not getting along."

With this sad declaration, I begin a concerted effort to win her back. I read David Deida's book, The Way of the Superior Man, a self-help volume with numerous suggestions on how to be the kind of man any woman would cherish. I entertain her, I cook for her, I take her out to concerts, Broadway plays and fine restaurants, I bring her morning coffee in bed, I avoid arguments, I do everything I can to win her back... and wait... and hope.

Two months later, we're having drinks at one of our favorite hangouts, and I ask her,

"So... how am I doing?"

She doesn't answer. I see her eyes welling up as she swallows hard.

"OMG, I just got the boot, didn't I?

173

"Not for the reason you think."

The details of the ensuing conversation are not important, only that she revealed her sexual preferences no longer involved men. There is little to say after a declaration like that. I experienced a whirlwind of emotions — incredulity, anger, surprise, relief, sadness, doubt, and even fear. My response reflected none of that. All I could muster up was,

"Oh..."

And that was that. Dr. Obadia must have known, and her insisting that I couldn't demand or even politely ask for sex should have informed me that something important had changed. I believe the street expression is "I had no gaydar." Multiple clues went right over my head, and with her sexual preference now declared, our eighteen-year marriage came to an end. There was no argument. How could there be? Though very sad, I felt some relief, as it was now clear that we weren't separating because I had done something unforgivable, other than being born with a Y chromosome.

Her realization had been brewing for quite a while. It was just too difficult for her to face it and own up. So, we both had to endure those painful months, her living with her realization and fear about how she would be perceived once the news was out; me, perplexed about what I had done that was so intolerable, it would end our marriage. Obviously, this situation would not be therapist-curable. My only choice — surrender, and get ready for yet another radical life change.

Though our marriage was over, the story has a happy ending, albeit with a couple of years of difficulty. We had two young boys who did not take the news well, and the result was some rough teenage years. But both have grown up to accept and embrace our choice to separate and explore new possibilities. To the relief of all, both boys have forged solid relationships with my ex, me, our new spouses, and their families.

Sometimes when we're working through difficulties, it appears that the odds are not "ever in our favor." Then we find the painful process was always in our best interests, removing us from an unworkable situation and freeing us up to find an ideal one. In my experience, this is true in marriage, friendships and careers.

To conclude this chapter, I must give credit and admiration to Dr. Obadia. Her insight and measured advice, though painful at the time, saved us from a much worse fate. Had I been allowed to request or even demand what my ex could not grant in good faith, the constant rejection would have caused my anger and resentment to undermine any chance of peaceful resolution. Fortunately, that did not happen. The pause also gave my ex the time she needed to face her fears about how friends and family might judge her and the change she was about to execute in her life's direction. In the end, we enjoyed a better outcome, despite it being quite different from anything I had envisioned!

Neelam

From Poland with Love

According to Buddha at the Gas Pump: *Neelam, a native of Poland, has been giving Satsang (spiritual teaching in a group with the goal of recognizing truth) internationally since 1996. Known for her simplicity, skillful discrimination, and intuitive insight, Neelam gently points toward the truth at the core of us all. With her extensive personal and teaching experience, she uses inquiry to facilitate her students in identifying and moving through deep-seated patterns of conditioning, bringing them to rest in Presence. Self-Inquiry is the core of this teaching and is based on Sri Ramana Maharshi's guidelines. Neelam's unique development of inquiry includes both recognizing our true nature and meeting our conditioning, with tenderness.*

I met Neelam in 2007, around the time my second marriage was falling apart. I was a mess. TM was still my go-to practice, but I needed some deep psyche scrubbing to see how I had managed to torpedo two marriages while coming from a family with no history of divorce. My friend Phil had been working with her, and was so enamored with her teaching and success rate helping people, he financed a promo video for her. I watched the video and was immediately sold, and signed up for a six-month intensive on the spot. Here's the story.

Phil is my go-to friend, since he knows my soon to be ex well. I'm falling apart and need help, so he recommends Neelam, because she is not only a spiritual teacher, she has vast knowledge and experience with mental health, depression and trauma. He invites me over and shows me a video of her answering tough questions from a group, and I like what I see. A six-month intensive with her is coming up that would comprise three in-person weekends, as well as satellite groups in the Northeast, in upstate New York, Boulder and Santa Fe that will work with her online between the live events. I'm just about to sign up for the Northeast group since I'm living on Long Island, but Phil makes an intriguing suggestion for something different. "Join the Colorado group instead. When it's over, we'll go skiing!" Now we're talking!

Fast forward: I'm at the home of Nina, one of the retreat participants near Boulder who has generously loaned her space to the group for retreat. My overall impression is it's wonderful. We're like a well-functioning family, something I am not used to! With guidelines for doing deep personal inquiry, we choose partners and work through our issues one by one as they arise. We also meditate in regular intervals, and Neelam calls in to discuss the day's events, giving her feedback and advice. There are tears, laughs, and often silence, again, very welcome considering my crazy life.

The first in-person event with Neelam comes around, and we are now sitting with her at the Mount Madonna Retreat Center in Watsonville, CA. After some introductions, to get the ball rolling,

I raise my hand. Neelam looks at me with a half-smile, half quizzical look, and says, "Yes?" I don't remember the question I asked, but it doesn't matter, because Neelam does not answer it. Instead, she replies,

"Jimmy... what do you really want?

With a resigned sigh, I say, "I want peace and spiritual enlightenment."

"Is that <u>all</u> you want?"

"Um...yes."

She smiles and says, "I don't think that's <u>all</u> you want."

"No, really. It is!"

"No, not really."

Then she disassembles my argument, and gently brings to my awareness (with some help from me) an array of worldly desires I want more, and on which I'm pursuing with a lot more determination than any spiritual aspirations. She does this with a compassionate, yet relentless interrogation, busting me wide open, almost to tears.

What I learn in this interaction is how I/we often act from the unconscious, fantasizing that we want one thing, but actually wanting another, while deluding ourselves that we are making progress in an area to which we are only paying lip service. This subtle interrogation opens me up like a primal scream, only softly, and with so much tenderness. After that, getting to feelings, worries, desires, as well as hidden and useless psycho-trash is considerably easier.

Neelam loves to sing, and towards the end of our first evening, she urges us to break out a guitar and do some songs. I knew nothing of this part of the

178

retreat, so I didn't bring a guitar. Another gentleman did, a man named Mark, but he's a beginner and limited in his musical abilities. Neelam suggests an appropriate song might be the Rolling Stones', "You Can't Always Get What You Want." Mark is having some trouble with the chords, so I jump on the opportunity to have some fun and ask,

"May I have a go?"

He says, slightly confused by my request, "Do you play guitar?"

"Yeah, I know a few chords."

Mark's a little reluctant to pass his guitar over to a stranger, but with a little hesitation, hands me his Yamaha acoustic.

No one except Phil knows I'm a professional, and he says nothing, enjoying the interaction and knowing what's coming. Mark hands me the guitar, and like the total showoff I can be sometimes, I tune it, and shred a few crazy riffs. I then begin the song with a dead accurate rendition of the original Stones intro.

I realize I'm sounding like a mischievous braggart, but damn, I'm enjoying the expressions on the group's faces as I execute the song exactly like the original recording. Everyone joins in singing, almost shouting the title line. It's a perfect expression of our experience on the retreat, and for many of us, especially me, spells out why we are here.

"You can't always get what you want."

"But if you try sometimes, you just might find ...you get what you need."

Neelam knows what she's doing.

Nothing to do after a rousing finale like that, so our evening ends. I sleep well that night, but a burning question arises from my Catholic years. Part of the supposition around sin is the notion of free will. If we have free will, then we may choose to be naughty or nice. According to this belief, our actions are our call, not fate or the hand of God. Teaching this belief is one way The Church tries to maintain order in a disorderly world. Through promulgating fear and guilt about our actions, the steep price for negative activity sinks in, and the reward could be a long stay at Hotel Inferno.

I'm not arguing with the church's motivation. We humans are a surly lot, and when the guardrails are removed, we tend to drift into entropy and start breaking things like horses in a hospital (borrowed from the comedian, John Mulaney). One could make the mistake of thinking the belief in heaven and hell would stop bad behavior in its tracks. Unfortunately, it doesn't. As I mentioned earlier, you can hop into a confessional any Saturday night and confess having just murdered the Queen and be absolved of your heinous act. Your punishment? A few Hail Marys and an Act of Contrition.

Of course I'm exaggerating, but the Catholics are not alone in this mindset. Eastern religions like Hinduism embrace the teachings of karma and reincarnation, where what you do, good or bad, comes back to you, either in this life or in a future one. From a scientific perspective, Isaac Newton's Third Law of Motion states, "For every action, there is an equal and opposite reaction." I like that theory from both physics and religion. It makes much more sense to me than one life to get it right, culminating in either harp plucking bliss or ass roasting agony. And, I'm well aware, dear reader, that many Christians hold this belief loosely, despite it being taught week after week in places of worship all over the world.

Getting back to our six-month course, I couldn't resist. I had to put the free will question to Neelam. If she is an enlightened master, surely, she'll have some sage insight into this dilemma. So here I go:

"Neelam..."

"Jimmy?"

"May I ask you about free will?"

"Of course."

"Is it real? Do we have free will?"

"Yes and no, depending on your perspective."

"Ok, let's start with I believe I have the free will to ask you this question."

"Really? And where did that thought come from?"

"From me. I thought of the question and asked."

"Yes, but again, where did that thought come from? What do you mean, from me?"

"The thought occurred to me, and I asked it."

"What do you mean, occurred to you?"

"Ok, well, the thought arose, and I asked the question."

"Arose from where?"

"I don't know. I had been thinking about it lately, and it just came up."

"From where?"

"From me. From my subconscious or wherever."

"The wherever is the important part of your statement. What does wherever mean to you?"

"I'm not sure. I don't know how or why thoughts arise. Maybe from a suggestion or something I heard.

"Sweetheart, it just arose. Thoughts arise from the silence deep inside of you. I call that Presence, your true nature. And on the deepest possible level, we are all one; we are all Presence. On the surface, it would appear that we have control. In ordinary life, without spiritual inquiry, we do not see the origin of our thoughts and ideas, and we assume we are making all of our own decisions. But if you look deeper, a different reality reveals itself." (Not an exact Neelam quote, but as close as I can remember)."

We went 'round and 'round with this, and one person became quite angry and agitated by what Neelam was suggesting. He just couldn't let it go, and as I recall, he never quite gave in. From my side, much as I wanted to think I was making choices like brushing my teeth or playing guitar, I fell silent, because I had no proof of either side of the argument.

For those unfamiliar with Presence, I would describe it as the silent, dimensionless void at the deepest level of our being, the infinite Self that looks out through our eyes and witnesses every thought, experience, emotion, and everything in existence. It is the most basic, fundamental "I." Maharishi calls it the source of thought. Science calls it the unified field. Because the experience of this unified field reveals its infinite, eternal nature, by definition, there can only be one of "it." Only one eternity (time) and one infinity (space) can logically exist. And any physicist will tell you, time is a made-up concept, so there goes eternity! Because of this oneness, we must all share that same infinite source, or that same unified self or Presence. Modern thinking in theoretical physics is beginning to gather around the idea that everything in the universe is this. Dr. Tony Nader, a neuroscientist and the current head of the TM movement, asserts that everything has its source in the unified field and the unified field of consciousness is the same as the unified field of physics. This is the principle of unity, as opposed to duality, the superficial observation of life I described a minute ago. In Indian philosophy, the study of this is called Advaita Vedanta.

But getting back to free will, Neelam's assertion, that in the deepest sense, there is no free will, has met with some scholarly disagreement. I recently attended a talk by Dr. John Hagelin, a theoretical physicist and president of Maharishi International University, who was asked that same question, do we have free will, and he said yes. We can make wise choices, or we can choose to do things that do not support our evolution as human beings, and those choices have their consequences. So, John's position leans more towards the Indian philosophy of karma and choice.

I leave you with this open question. Does it matter who is right? If we have no free will, we will still make choices, whether they are our own or those of Providence. And if we do have free will, again, we will continue to make our day-to-day choices. So, beyond creating lively arguments at the pub, the subject itself will probably be of less interest to the average person, than the price of eggs or the evening news.

Aside from reinforcing what I had learned and observed from my years of TM, Neelam taught a principle that stands out from much of what this book has covered — the principal of tenderness. We can be so merciless with ourselves when we make mistakes. Our superego can be a harsh judge, the source of so much insecurity, and, as I pointed out earlier, an always-on opinion monger. When dealing with this uncomfortable mental nonsense, Neelam taught us to, in the words of the song, "Try a Little Tenderness." The issues that assail us in this lifetime can be very difficult, but we can make the job of resolving them so much easier if we could just be tender with ourselves. That's certainly how she was with me. It worked wonders in bringing me around and opening me up.

Another approach to conflict I learned from her was something that might seem obvious to many, but went right over my head — the difference between response and reaction. I had a situation that was getting the best of me — constant conflict with a coworker, and when I described how I was handling it with little success, she asked me a baffling question:

"Why are you reacting to everything he says? Wouldn't it be better to respond?"

I wasn't sure what she was talking about. She described reaction as firing back in the moment with little thought and often intending to dominate or even hurt someone. Response means taking a moment to digest what had been said, thinking it through, and commenting in a way that brings some resolution as opposed to escalation. It takes presence of mind to do that, and it can be difficult when triggered, but it makes a substantial difference in how an argument proceeds.

The trigger part is key. When we are triggered, it can be very difficult to do anything but fire back. But… it is possible when we know an argument is about to ensue, to recognize the volatility of the situation, gather our wits, and emotionally prepare for the storm. If you can do that, then it is far easier to hold your temper and respond. Be careful though. I find it's possible to speak with faux restraint, pretending to respond, while introducing passive aggression, spoken in a calm but condescending voice that will be interpreted as anything but a response!

I spent two years working with Neelam. But eventually we have to leave our schools and teachers and set out on our own, hopefully putting what we learned to good use. I'll admit this is a work in progress for me, but I am eternally grateful for what I learned from Neelam. If you are interested in working with her, she teaches in Santa Fe, NM and can be contacted through her website at Neelam.org.

Hypnotic Regression

When I was a kid, my family and I used to watch the Ed Sullivan show every Sunday night. It was always fun seeing my heroes perform — one night it would be Elvis; Another, the Beatles, and still another, Buddy Holly or crazy Victor Borge, the hilarious piano virtuoso comic. If you're not familiar, Google him. There are many videos of his antics on YouTube. But a different variety of non-musical entertainers also fascinated me — the hypnotists. I remember gathering around our old 50s black and white Sylvania TV, my sister, my mom, my dad and me, squashed together on the couch, watching in awe as a Las Vegas hypnotist induced a grown man into a trance and instructed him to squat down, flap his arms and quack like a duck. Without expression, the man obliged, oblivious to the roaring laughter from the live audience. Then, when the hypnotist snapped his fingers, the man would wake up clueless of his folly. I half-believed what I saw, but not enough to consider trying it myself.

Fast forward to the twenty-first century. One evening, while scrolling through books on my iPad Kindle reader, I stumbled upon a curious title that tickled my spiritual bent, Journey of Souls, by Dr. Michael Newton. The introduction revealed Newton's unusual discoveries, incorporating hypnotism into psychotherapy and making some astonishing discoveries regarding reincarnation and life between lives. Here's some background on the author from the Newton Institute website:

"Dr. Newton was an acclaimed international spiritual regressionist, who discovered how to enable people to access the wisdom of the spirit world and their higher guidance while living their lives. Known as a pioneer of afterlife exploration, his dedicated research over 30 years mapped for us insight into our Life Between Lives (LBL) ® as presented in his books, Journey of Souls and Destiny of Souls."

Dr. Newton used hypnotism to probe the depths of consciousness, hoping to help people resolve difficult issues that other therapies found illusive. It all began when, during an ordinary hypnotic regression, a patient described personal events that took place prior to their birth. This was unheard of in hypnotherapy or any but the most occult studies, so he began regressing his patients further and further into their past and found multiple patients reporting similar events. His life and extraordinary work are chronicled at NewtonInstitute.org.

After reading *Journey of Souls,* I became obsessed with gaining more knowledge about this crazy discovery. If I could trace the origins of my life conditions, parents, family members, friends, etc., it would confirm my suspicion that I had a choice in how my current life would unfold. Like the victim scenario described in the EST chapter, I sensed I was not thrown into my life circumstances without some decision making on my part. It wasn't a deeply held belief, per se. It just seemed like a possibility worth exploring.

Session 1

The Newton website contained a list of trained practitioners, so I scanned it to see if there was one nearby. To my amazement, I found a Newton Institute Certified LBL therapist in my hometown, a gentleman named Billy Hunter. Not only did he have the skills I was seeking, his Facebook page revealed we had many friends in common. I called and booked him for September 13, 2017. Here's the remarkable story:

I arrive at 1PM. Billy Hunter meets me at the door and escorts me to a warmly decorated study with a reclining chair/bed, a desk, and an office chair. A portable recorder and a pad and pen are nearby on the coffee table. We chat for about ten minutes, getting acquainted and sharing our list of common friends. With that conversation complete, we begin.

He briefs me on what will transpire during the next few hours. Because I'm a little nervous, I miss a lot of what he is saying. He's used to that and says, "Don't worry about remembering any of this. It will make more sense once we go through the complete procedure."

Then he instructs me to close my eyes and relax.

Hypnotizing a patient is more involved than I have the space to describe, so the following will be a summary rather than a blow-by-blow description of the process.

After inducing me into a hypnotic trance, he says, "We will now go back to a pleasant memory from when you were a young boy."

In a soft and friendly voice, he says, "Join me in a descent back in time — five... four... three... two... When I put my hand on your forehead we will be there in that wonderful time and place... ONE."

I am now in a trance like the Ed Sullivan volunteer, but something is different. I'm both present in the moment and also an observer of the moment. It's unclear how I transitioned from Billy's office to six years old, but I am now looking at myself on Christmas morning, surrounded by presents in a joyous and exciting moment. It is 1952.

Billy takes me deeper. "Three, two, one." I witness a recurring childhood nightmare. We pause to explore the scene, but we don't dwell on it. Then deeper, "three, two, one." I'm in my mother's womb. She's anxious that she'll die in childbirth, and I sense her distress. I kick to distract her. She loves my life's energy inside her and snaps out of it. I joined this fetus at around six months (not at conception, as some might believe). I go more deeply into this in Part II.

A quick note here: this was not my imagination. It was an experience, much like being there in that moment, a memory as clear as what I had for breakfast. We continue:

Billy directs me to "the light," then a "tunnel back in time" to an important lifetime. He counts down from ten to one as I go speeding through the tunnel. The walls get lighter. He instructs that on "one," I am to find myself outside in an important previous lifetime. Then he whispers, "one..."

Billy required no previous belief in reincarnation. I agreed to follow the directions as best I could, and we'd see what shook out. If I arrived at nothing, I'm not sure what we would do. We didn't need to put that to the test.

I am standing outdoors on a dirt street. We are in a small Texas town, and the year is 1876. Dressed in a religious frock, I see that I'm a missionary priest, and I'm engaged in a serious conversation with a beautiful, elegantly-dressed woman. She is a close friend, but not a Catholic, and she asks, "Why do you continue to be a priest? Is it serving any useful purpose or helping anyone to whom you minister?" Her question makes me feel sick. I'm hiding something. My eyes tear up as I stare at the ground, depressed and debilitated.

She admonishes me.

"You are a hypocrite, preaching spiritual ecstasy through your Christ, though you are without joy yourself."

But her tone is soft. She's more like a friend coming to my rescue. Though we have a loving relationship, we are not romantically involved.

The bigger picture now reveals itself. In this lifetime, I am a notorious hardcore bible basher. My parish dislikes me, and I'm having a difficult time convincing myself or anyone else that what I preach is relevant, effective, or even true. She agrees, saying,

"Your work is a waste of time."

I remember with anger and regret, I let my father coerce me into joining the priesthood. He told me it was God's will, that I had no choice and like a fool, I believed him. My friend is correct. I am a hypocrite. I never wanted to be a priest.

The scene changes, and now I'm sitting on a wooden step in front of an old western building. I break down and cry. (I also start crying in Billy's office). The woman lays her hand on my shoulder, consoling me. She's like an angel, with kindness in her eyes, deep understanding and pure love.

The scene shifts again, and I am now fifty-five years old. I've resigned from the priesthood, rudderless and lost. With little means of support, all I can afford is a cheap, flimsy, frontier style cabin built by unskilled pioneers. The floors and walls often creak when the wind picks up, making the house seem alive, and not in a good way. This night, a thunderstorm is raging outside, and a powerful gust of wind pummels the house with enough force to dislodge a poorly anchored overhead beam. I hear a crack, and as I look up, the beam slips off the joist, crashing down on my head, killing me instantly.

There is no pain, just blissful silence as I rest in the beautiful light of this alternate dimension. Overwhelming joy and relief fill my being — I am happy to end that miserable life and transition to the next.

Billy asks, "Do you have any regrets?"

"None. The experience relieved me of ever wanting to be a priest again."

We often hear of near-death experiences where we are met by deceased family members and friends, welcoming us to the afterlife. I have no such experience. I see that my greeting is coming from a group of purple-robed elders. They exude love and kindness, and I realize I am not a stranger, but one of them. We all know each other well. They are my people, unlike my earth family, who are just acquaintances in the afterlife. As I look at each, I see an almost blinding orange light emanating from them. We have been around for eons.

Billy asks, "How many lifetimes?"

"10,956. I'm worried that I'm making this stuff up,"

Billy encourages me to not judge or analyze.

"Just be in the moment, and let it flow, wherever it may go."

"You're right. Where would I get ideas like this? Not from my Catholic upbringing! The church would have me meeting Christ and St. Peter at the Pearly Gates!"

I am conscious and awake in a hypnotic trance, and there's a strong possibility that I'm experiencing genuine far-memory.

Ego issues have plagued me for lifetimes. In my LBL conference with the elders, they remind me I designed my current lifetime to help me overcome my conceit. With this revelation, it's clear why I find myself, "Always the best man, never the groom." My accomplishments, though impressive to some, always seem to fall short of my goals and expectations. I wanted to be a rock star. Instead, my talents were limited by a spiritual restraining order, humbling me and relegating me to the background, helping others to achieve their goals, but rarely being able to achieve my own. Now, it all makes sense.

Billy encourages me to let this new knowledge marinate, and we move on. I shift to another previous lifetime. We're now in the early 1900s, and I am a World War 1 fighter pilot for the Deutsche Luftstreitkräfte, or in English, The Imperial German Air Service. My specialty is marauding in biplanes equipped with bombs and some limited guns. I'm good at what I do, but my ego is out of control. Women find me handsome. I'm first in my class, a skilled pilot, and a lady's man extraordinaire. On the darker side, I'm dispassionate, boastful, and careless. While on a sortie, I get distracted, and an unseen Sopwith Camel from the British Royal Flying Corps shoots me down. My narcissistic life ends at twenty-five years old.

Upon my arrival in the LBL, the elders are not happy. We had designed this German lifetime to be long and filled with deep learning and spiritual development. While I may have gained expert knowledge in the material realm, I squandered my privilege and intelligence on warring and womanizing.

They help me understand that my current lifetime results from wasting the previous one. They/we limited fame and success, but provided abundant resources for spiritual development and learning. I'm ok with that. This scenario wasn't much fun growing up, but it is what I needed.

With my inquiry into this lifetime complete, I become silent, waiting for further instructions. Billy says, "Much has been gained in this time... a lot of perspective and understanding... all that you are, all that you've been. Now it's time to conclude our journey. But before we do, see if there's something that feels like unfinished business, something that would be good to review before we come back."

I search my memories for an answer... then laugh and say, "Enlightenment, spiritual enlightenment. That was supposed to happen in the German lifetime, but I got seduced by the dark side of the force — wine, women and warring. They yanked me out of that lifetime at twenty-five and sent me back after a short thirty earth years to take another crack at it this lifetime. Since my youth, the opportunities for spiritual and psychological growth keep hitting me in the face like stepping on a rake."

Billy says, "You can allow this understanding, this knowingness to stay. Everything you've gained in our short time together will remain with you. Let us come back, back to this present time, bringing it all forward with you. And to come back, I'm going to count one last time, bringing you back so eyes can be open. I'll count from one up to ten this time. When I reach ten, you'll feel my hand on your forehead one last time, and you can open your eyes. And when you do, you're going to feel awake, refreshed and clear, and you're going to feel better than you've felt in a long time."

He begins the counting procedure, giving instruction and assurance with each successive number. On ten, with his hand on my head, I slowly open my eyes, yawn and stretch. He hands me a glass of water as I glance at my watch. In my trance-warped sense of time, I am certain I had only been under for about a half hour, maybe forty-five minutes. I am astounded to find it's 3 PM, two hours later. We chat for another ten minutes. I get up, thank him, and making my way to the door, I head home.

Through this hypnotic regression, I finally solved a mystery that had plagued me my entire life. In my twenties, I realized I had some egoic delusions. That was obvious, but the cause eluded me. My life and achievements weren't so special that I had anything to be arrogant or conceited about. If we look at a sliding scale ego chart, with humility on one end and narcissism on the other, much of my life would be near the middle, just a tad on the narcissistic or at least egotistical side. Add insecurity and depression to the mix, and you can see why I've spent so much time and effort searching for a cure for this uncomfortable mental state in which I've spent much of my life.

Did learning about the previous lifetimes which led to my current problems cure them? Nope. Again, let's not confuse knowledge with action. One doesn't grow and develop by thinking about growing and developing — no work, no progress. However, getting a glimpse into my far past made it easier to accept when my career work failed or went unnoticed, or my personal interactions were less than stellar. It helped diffuse the resentment I had often felt in the past when things didn't go my way. What feels right to me is I am responsible for the strange way my life has succeeded with little recognition.

I'm willing to consider that I may have planned the outcome before I was born, and this plan has helped to tamp down my egoistic tendencies and stubborn religious myopia. It's been a humbling journey.

Ok, back to hypnotic regression. With this little two-hour taste, I'm eager to dig deeper, so Billy suggests a second session. We make an appointment for a week later, September 21, 2017. Read on for part two.

Session 2

In this session, we paid a second visit to my German lifetime, but this time, we delved much more deeply into meaning. The regressions became quite personal. Almost every scene illustrated missteps and bad choices, no matter the scenario. I took it all in, trying to stay positive and not let it get me down.

September 21, 2017

We begin the session with a step-by-step regression similar to the previous week. This time, Billy asks for more detail at each landing, and I tell him what I see. The images and recollections are fascinating to me, but unimportant in the bigger picture of this amazing process. I will spare you the less interesting personal details and get to the revelations that caused me some emotional upheaval, and were as amazing as anything I read in Journey of Souls.

Arriving on the next landing of the hypnotic regression, we pause, and again, like last week, I find myself back in the womb. Billy wants more detail this time around.

"What do you see? What do you feel?"

"I hear my mom's stomach gurgling, and it makes me feel happy and not alone."

But then, as described in the chapter, Hypnotic Regression Part One, I sense her anxiety. Billy asks me to explain.

Some quick background: My mother's doctor told her if she had one more child, she could die in childbirth. This thought haunted and terrified her throughout her pregnancy. The doctor was wrong. She had an easy pregnancy physiologically if not psychologically and an even easier delivery. But to continue...

Somehow, my consciousness is functioning far better than I would expect at this developmental stage. I'm perplexed that I'm in a situation where I must be the adult — she is behaving like a vulnerable child. To her, my presence in her womb is wonderful, yet she believes me to be the harbinger of death. I kick to snap her out of her morbid fantasy, hoping she'll cease her delusions.

We move on. A sense of strength and power fills my being. I'm about to be born into an important but challenging lifetime. In the LBL, the robed elders voiced concern that this body may not support my ambitions. I won't be handsome this time. My eyesight will be slightly better than a bat, encumbering me with thick glasses — no chance of being a pilot. Career success is a possibility, but nothing like the German lifetime. As I mentioned in Part 1, these limitations were my choice. They are not a punishment. I chose them to help me focus on spiritual evolution, not partying.

Billy says, "Let's revisit your German fighter pilot's lifetime. (He counts, three, two, one...) Now, please ignore all the adulation and glory, and tell me why you are here?"

Because I spent five lifetimes as a Catholic priest in sexual handcuffs (unfortunately, not the kinky kind), and I wanted to have some fun before getting back to work.

My name is Hans, and observing my surroundings, I see I'm at a formal ball in a palace. I believe we are in Austria. The walls are a pale white, adorned with gold trim around every window and alcove. The floor is covered in a ruby-red carpet. A huge oval-shaped dome painting expands over most of the ceiling, depicting a pleasant pastoral scene. People mill about with drinks in hand. Servers scurry through the crowd carrying trays of refills and collecting empties. All attendees are enjoying lively conversations, and everyone is dressed in formal attire — women in long, brightly colored gowns, men in the usual black tie and tails. A violinist, violist and harpist play softly in the background. This evening, I am basking in celebrity status. It's not clear what I've done to deserve it, only that I'm the center of attention. I'm enjoying the men congratulating me and the beautiful women surrounding me, flirting and vying for my attention. But then a particular woman catches my eye.

In the present, still in a hypnotic trance, I recognize her. She's the same woman from my devastating lifetime as a Texas priest. But as the German pilot in the encounter, I do not know why she holds my attention. She just seems disturbingly familiar. In reality, she is my friend and provocateur from the past and we are facing each other again across lifetimes. It wasn't good the last time, and I'm pretty sure it won't be this time.

I experience an unsettling chill. There's little that frightens me these days, but I can't deny that her look seems to indicate something is wrong. This young, *beautiful woman has locked her steel-blue eyes on mine like a fortune teller who has uncovered a devastating event on the horizon. A fellow officer notices my changed demeanor. To distract me from my obvious concern, he smiles, and with a wink and encouraging tone, he says,*

"She's British royalty, Hans! Looks like she has you in her sights! Go get her, my friend." I am unimpressed and have no desire to approach her.

Of interest in hypnosis is the opportunity to have two simultaneous perspectives. For me, I am Jimmy in Billy's office, and also Hans in the early 1900s. In the present, I sense the woman was far more than an attractive young aristocrat at a jubilant affair. In this turn of the century scenario, I'm disturbed by her presence but not sure why. Here on Billy's couch, I see her attendance at this ball is not an accident — she is there to warn me there is grave danger in my immediate future. How have I come to this dramatic conclusion regarding what seems to be just a cold stare? Is my imagination going overboard then and now? I will soon learn she is the Angel of Death in a scarlet gown. So how do I respond in the moment? I'm a narcissistic clod, so mentally, I give her the one-finger salute, break off the stare-down, and go back to my womanizing!

But inside something has changed. Somehow, with her cold, piercing stare, she has stirred some of my darkest emotions, uncovering my insecurities, fears, and vulnerability. Though I try to ignore the uneasy feeling, my brief encounter with this woman has left me shaken. The interaction seems significant to both Billy and me, so we agree to dig deeper.

After our silent interaction, I didn't see her again. World War 1 was about to begin, and I had to get back to Germany.

Death

Details about my travel back to the fatherland, preparation for war, and the surrounding events did not come up in our session. We moved directly to the last moments of my life, and I resumed my exploration. Eyes closed, deep in hypnotic trance, I reveal what I see:

Flying high over Istrana (Italy), I'm lost in my thoughts, basking in the glory of having just shot down several enemy planes. The sleek wings of my Fokker D-VII, cut through the clouds on this glorious spring day. Our D-VIIs are the pride of the Imperial German Air Service — formidable fighters, painted in seven-color camouflage and emblazoned with Maltese Crosses on the wings and fuselage. I'm beaming with pride, holding the joystick loosely in my right hand without a care in the world.

In my self-congratulatory daze, I am unaware of a menacing presence shadowing me. A Sopwith Camel, the double wing flagship of the British Air Command, is lining up, and I am in his cross-sights.

I'm awakened from my daydream by the faint hum of a second airplane engine. It's coming from my blind spot, behind and under my starboard tail wing... my mind explodes!

"Verdammte scheiße! A fucking Brit is tailing me!"

I squeeze the throttle, revving my engine to full power and try to maneuver, but I can't lose him. I dive, I climb, I bank left, then a hard right, but it's as if he's attached to my plane with a tow rope. Then, over my engine noise and through the ear covers of my leather helmet, I hear an ear-piercing rat-a-tat-tat. A hail of bullets tears through my wings, my fuselage... and me. Terror and agony envelop me as I comprehend what has happened. I'm hit... I'm bleeding... I have no parachute... It's over.

Now in tatters, my biplane spirals downward in a trail of smoke and flames. I am losing consciousness as I bleed out and watch the ground approaching. Then, BOOM, my journey ends, slamming into a hill, exploding on impact. My death is instantaneous. But... I am conscious, experiencing neither pain nor fear. At first, I don't know where I am or what is happening, only that it's dazzling and beautiful. Not what I expected. With my recent past, I would have anticipated something dark and hot. Then it all becomes clear. I'm back. I remember this place from being here many times before. I have entered the realm of life between lives.

In the ensuing post-mortem moments, I learn my demise is not an accident. An authority higher than the British Air Command has extracted me from this Roman orgy murder-fest. I have been called home, out of the game. Like the near-death experiences we hear and read about, I feel carefree and blissful floating in the light. With a laugh, I protest to no one in particular, "Oh, come on! I was just getting started." Talk about unrepentant.

The fun and pleasure of this lascivious lifetime were welcome after my five-life sentence in pathetic priesthoods, so no regrets. But some karma remains. I realize in the present, under Billy Hunter's guidance, that my desire for that high octane action and excitement hasn't fully waned. It has followed me into this current lifetime, though with several restrictions.

Life Between Lives

We explored the crash in both sessions, and mentioned some between life insights, but now we go into greater detail about the aftermath.

So, I'm back in the bright golden light, beautiful beyond words. But I'm unable to enjoy this extraordinary environment. Instead, I'm feeling disappointed and serious. Now, detached from Hans, realization sets in that I wasted a precious lifetime, killing and getting laid. Under current circumstances, the egotistical glory and self-congratulations seem absurd. Though I may have had some justification for the killings as a soldier, i.e. "just following orders," here in the in-between lives, I'm experiencing deep regret and sadness for the many young men I sent plummeting to their death.

Within a short time after my entry into the LBL, I am approached by an older looking gentleman who says,

"Welcome back, Kamir." (Apparently, that is my spirit name in this dimension)

"Now that you've gotten all that nonsense out of your system, are you ready to get some work done?"

He is Kamal, my senior guide. We know each other well. I notice a touch of sarcasm in his tone. Unlike newer souls, I've reincarnated thousands of times, and no one is coddling me. Those with my experience are held to quite high standards, and it is clear I have fallen a little short. That's a cosmic understatement. One of my main pre-incarnation goals in this past lifetime was to "wake up" in the spiritual sense. If anything, I spent twenty-five years doing just the opposite.

We chat for a while, then Kamal suggests I take some time to relax and reorient to my spirt-world surroundings. No one is rushing, everyone is chill and cheerful, so I set out to reconnect with old friends and family members. This dimension is very different from life on earth. Here we are all spirits. There are no siblings, children, or parents per se. Those are relationships we take on during an incarnation to work out karma and grow. My mother in one lifetime could be my daughter or son in another. Friends here could also choose to be mortal enemies on earth if it serves to resolve previous lifetime conflicts or help either party in their evolution. As I mix and mingle, I'm reminded of the love we all share for each other here and how we volunteer to create earth relationships that bring us closer to realization of the higher beings we are at our core.

It feels good to be out of my dense, time/space-limited body. My turn-of-the-century vacation has ended, and I'm ready to move on.

The rest of our session focused on my plans for this current lifetime, the limitations I agreed to embody, and my exploration into spiritual enlightenment. We also uncovered the memory of a life review that took place but was nothing like my childhood fears. For those expecting reassurance about their religious beliefs, I have disappointing news for you — St. Peter neither summoned a flock of angels to float me up to heaven, nor assembled a gaggle of demons to drag me clawing and screaming down into hell for eternal torture. In fact, St. Peter and Beelzebub were no-shows! Here's what happened:

As with my previous lifetimes, a council of elders assembles in a large tent, each taking their place behind a long table or bench, as it's called in courts. A woman in the center position appears to be the spokesperson for the inquiry. Standing before these nine judges and accompanied by Kamal, who stands behind me as my advocate, we review what I accomplished on my German holiday. My inquisitors are neither harsh nor judgmental. All are understanding, emanating love and kindness combined with genuine concern about my well-being but also being firm that the party is over. There is some back and forth about my goals and aspirations and what can be done next time to achieve them. They warn me that a human lifetime is precious, and it would not be wise to waste another. Turning away from the light again could have serious consequences. But even their warnings are soft and given with love. I feel more coached than blamed.

As Billy and I continue our exploration into my LBL, a mind-blowing event comes to light, which draws us into an experience beyond anything I have ever imagined.

Upon completion of my life review, Kamal says, "I would like to give you a glimpse of an ego-free condition where your consciousness clears and your true identity reveals itself in all its shining glory. This experience will be very helpful in your next lifetime."

Many saints attest to this experience of ultimate clarity, so I have an intellectual idea of what might be coming. But I soon learn he is planning on taking this further than I would like. He introduces the possibility of evolving to a state of no self, which, for most people, would be terrifying. With some trepidation, I agree to the lesson, but he doesn't warn me about the involvement of a death-defying challenge — not quite an ambush, but not quite full disclosure either. The lesson begins:

I'm not sure where we are, how we got here, or what is to come, but we are standing near the edge of a sheer cliff. This impossibly high precipice looms above God knows what — I can only see nothingness. There are no clouds, no fog, not even blue sky; only empty space. It is as unsettling as my worst nightmares, and I am regretting my decision to come here. Kamal remains a few feet behind me, calm as ever. When I turn to question him, I notice we are not alone. A tall, radiant being has joined us. She smiles, but says nothing. With both of them now standing behind me, and the cliff in front of me, I am certain that something unpleasant is about to happen. With a shaky voice, I inquire, "Why are we here? What is going on?"

Without a word to allay my fears, our radiant companion performs an extraction that is so abstract, I have great difficulty understanding it. With a sweeping gesture, she gathers my ego, removing it from my ethereal body and holds it tightly in her arms. Then, in a cheerful and enthusiastic voice, she commands,

"Go! Leap from the cliff! You are safe. There is no danger."

"Are you crazy? How can I be safe? You're asking me to commit suicide! Is this the final punishment for my despicable past lifetime?"

She smiles, shaking her head, and says, "No, dear one. You will be safe. Just go."

I want to believe her, but as I stand at the edge of the cliff, staring into the void, I am paralyzed with fear. Again, she urges,

"Go, beloved! Take this leap of faith. You will come to no harm. There is something wonderful waiting for you. You have my word."

I take one last anxious look at this radiant being, my ego in her arms, and with a deep breath, step off the cliff into infinite space. In an instant, my terror is transformed into astonishment. There appears to be no gravity, so I do not plummet to a horrible death. Instead, I float away into the blackest darkness I have ever experienced. This boundless void is neither frightening nor nightmarish, just calm and pleasant. All of my lifetimes, everything I have ever known or experienced has been left behind in the arms of an angel, and my mind is blank. I experience only presence — no thoughts, no memories, just silent, pure existence. It is not "other," something that I am witnessing as an observer, nor is it a mental state or temporary lapse of memory. I am awake in the deepest state of my being — the fundamental me — who I am under all the layers of memory, ideas, illusions, traumas, disappointments and desires. My true identity now unfolds as immense, eternal, infinite, no beginning, no end, silent, pure being. I don't try to figure out any of this — where I am or what is happening, because there is no "me" to figure anything out. There is no self. In stark contrast to what one might fear or imagine, I'm at ease and comfortable. All disillusionment is gone. I am home. It is wonderful beyond measure, so I float silently in the void, basking in the blissful stillness.

I could remain here forever, but my earth body is still on the couch in Billy's office. To my disappointment, I remember flesh and blood are defined by boundaries and subject to the limitations of time and space. This incredible experience, like all things, must pass. Eyes still closed, I twitch and frown with this realization, and that is the cue.

Billy reminds me it's time to come back to waking conscious, time to end my hypnotic regression. The experience left me in tears on the couch. I don't know why, because I felt a wonderful sense of lightness and joy. I could only describe it as ultimate freedom and pure ecstasy. To say no worries would be the understatement of the century. Still, it had me weeping, and as such, a little embarrassed. Billy assured me my reaction was quite normal with an experience like this and handed me the box of tissues.

Digging or exploring further made little sense after this peak experience, so with sequential steps and placing his hand on my forehead, Billy brought me out of trance. I stretched, wiped my tears and had a drink of water as we chatted about all we had uncovered. With a broad smile, he assured me he captured every word on the recording to reference and enjoy any time I liked.

A few months later Billy informed me that my story would be included in the next Book by Michael Newton called *Destiny of Souls – 70 Case Histories of LBL Regressions.* At first, I felt a little embarrassed that my personal revelations would be exposed to the world in a popular book series, but then he told me they would change my name for the story. I had to laugh. Once again, fame without the recognition! In this case, I was fine with that decision.

Aftermath

Later that year, on a retreat with a spiritual teacher named Adyashanti, the "no self" experience returned, this time during full waking consciousness. I enjoyed this incredible identity shift for three long days. Imagine walking around the resort grounds, eating in the cafeteria with friends, meditating, listening to lectures… with no self. The absence of worry, daydreaming, regret, resentment, endless mind chat, and fear created an incredible feeling of lightness and joy. Just the release from worry alone would be enough, but this identity shift redefined freedom. The term mindless is considered a derogatory term, but we must not conflate mindless, i.e. irresponsibility, with mindless, no self. One creates chaos, the other creates order and bliss. As such, I look forward to my next experience of mindful mindlessness! And I would be fine with it becoming permanent. That is the goal. That is enlightenment.

Conclusion

There will always be more to this ongoing story, as human evolution never ceases from birth to death. Whether we seek help or go it alone, we grow, if not actively, then passively. Some people avoid self-inquiry and just carry on with their lives. Maybe they're miserable but have neither access nor the finances to pursue a path of recovery. Maybe they're unhappy but don't believe in or are suspicious of outside help. No matter how hard we try to keep it all bottled up or nailed down, nature has a way of presenting challenges that change even the most hardcore Vulcans. That lover that leaves us because they just couldn't take it anymore, whatever "it" was? That job from which we just got fired? That promotion that someone else received, and we didn't? That election we lost? These experiences unfold as lessons in a constant stream, whether we learn from them or not. If we didn't learn, nature is happy to reschedule the lesson down the road, over and over, until we master the subject. The Universe does not require the wise counsel of a therapist or teacher to prescribe evolutionary lessons. She dishes out the curriculum, and we get schooled. It's just quicker and less painful if we take some initiative and get help.

With every challenge, success or failure, there is *some* growth. Maybe it's tiny, unnoticeable, maybe it's just a memo from the universe that says,

"Are you sure you don't want to examine that interaction and see if next time you might do better?

Do you really want to stick your finger in that electric socket... *again?*"

This mental voice speaks to us in words, images and emotions, daily with or without outside coaching.

I submit it is impossible to go through life on earth and learn nothing about your motivations, your fears or your shortcomings, despite what it might look like to others. Pain and discomfort are powerful motivators. Our tendency is to move away from pain and towards happiness, i.e. looking for love, seeking fun, entertainment, relief, sex, sports, more sleep, more vacation time, and innumerable other outward-focused activities. It is the natural tendency of the mind.

Seeking happiness can also take the form of hideous behavior, the need to cause others pain, abuse, murder, rape, etc., why? Because somewhere inside, we feel that doing such things will make us happier, or at the very least, relieve our misery. But in my experience, it is the inward-focused work that delivers the lasting results.

I sat as long as I could on the holdout bleachers, but by eighteen, I had to admit I did not have the tools to make the pain go away. Natural evolution alone was not cutting it for me. My brief encounter with recreational chemicals didn't produce desirable results, either. No regrets. I have been blessed with both the motivation and the means to explore and heal myself, and with the writing of this book, I attest to the efficacy of this work.

I wish I was qualified to recommend specific therapies for whatever ails my readers as do writers and teachers like Eckhart Tolle, Tony Robbins,

Werner Erhard, or Krishnamurti, but as I've said from the beginning, I am not a psychiatrist, psychologist, guru or psychic. I do, however, feel comfortable making one recommendation — you can start from wherever you are. If you seek happiness in a positive, life-affirming way, then take the first step. Ask a friend, read a book by a self-development expert... *do something*. I've found that simply having the desire to get better can create a path to recovery. You may not see that path right away, but if your intention and desire are strong, maybe a book drops in your lap like it did for me. Maybe a friend will relate an experience that starts you thinking. Maybe you just go on the internet and book a session with a therapist or social worker, take a yoga class, learn how to meditate, anything, but the first step is the desire to change the status quo. Then you must get off the couch and act.

I urge you, dear reader, to take that first step. Don't accept unhappiness as a given, even though it may seem inevitable. You have the right to live in a happy, peaceful state of being that is unshakable by life's difficulties. It is within your reach, even if the transformation may not be immediate. Yes, it may require time and work, but the time will pass, anyway. If you begin the process of self-healing now, in five years, you will see progress. If you don't start, you may be in much the same mental state as you were five years ago, or worse, still not enjoying life the way you could have been.

If unhappiness is your state, know that you are not alone, nor is your situation hopeless. There have been pioneers throughout time who have mapped out paths to bliss. They have documented their discoveries, and in this digital age, those paths are accessible to anyone with a desire, a computer or smartphone, an internet connection, or a library card.

I am not naïve and don't deny there are those whose lives are a living hell. For these poor souls, there may not be enough awareness to conceive of a cure other than death itself. My heart goes out to them, and recommendations for their dilemmas are way beyond the scope of this book. I speak to the rest of us, the people living ordinary lives, in ordinary situations in varying degrees of emotional discomfort. To all of you, I send my love and encouragement to open your minds if you haven't already done so, and consider that you are what you think, and what you think can change your life for the better or the worse. How you live your life is up to no one but you. If the darkness feels like it's closing in, don't just sit there. Don't accept that mental nonsense. Get up. Get going on whatever it takes to heal your broken heart. I hope that this book serves as a collection of ideas, ordinary and bizarre, that inspires you to set out on your own journey towards creating a life of fulfillment and happiness.

Jimmy Ryan
April 5, 2025

www.ingramcontent.com/pod-product-compliance
Lightning Source LLC
Chambersburg PA
CBHW070608100426

42744CB00006B/430